D1468606

DON'T TREAD ON ME!

The Constitution and State Sovereignty

Copyright © 2009 by Paul Curtman

Published by Greatheart Publishing
2025 Skyline Dr. Suite 101
Pacific, MO 63069

Printed in the United States of America
ISBN: 978-0-9814524-2-5

For bulk discounts, please contact the author at:
www.paulcurtman.com or paulcurtman@gmail.com

*Without the encouragement of my parents,
this book would not have been written.*

When the righteous are in authority, the people rejoice: but
when the wicked beareth rule, the people mourn.

– Prov 29:2

In God I will praise his word, in God I have put my trust;
I will not fear what flesh can do unto me.

– Psa 56:4

CONTENTS

Introduction vii

The Gadsden Flag 1

1. The Declaration of Independence and Individual Sovereignty 5

2. State Sovereignty 15

3. The Preamble to the Constitution 21

4. Article 1 Section 3
   State Sovereignty and US Senators 29

5. Article 1 Section 8
   The Enumerated Powers of the Legislative Branch 37

6. Article 2 Section 2
   US Senators and Treaties 49

7. Article 4 Section 4
   A Nation of Sovereign Republics 55

8. The 9th and 10th Amendments and State Sovereignty 61

9. The Chains of the Constitution 71

10. Original Intent - Valuable Quotes from Our Founding Fathers ... 83

    The Declaration of Independence 107

    The US Constitution 113

INTRODUCTION

Among the Founding Fathers of American government, there are two that stand out from the rest. One of those men is Thomas Jefferson, the author of the Declaration of Independence. It was Thomas Jefferson who, in a few short days, penned one of the most remarkable declarations of the rights of man the world has ever known. The other one is James Madison who is often called the Father of the Constitution. It was Madison who introduced the new plan for American government at the Constitutional Convention in Philadelphia. Madison also kept minutes during the debates that took place while the Constitution was being drafted. He also authored many of the *Federalist Papers* to explain the Constitution and encourage its ratification.

When investigating the principles in the Declaration of Independence and the original intent of their application into our Constitution, the thoughts of Jefferson and Madison may very well provide the most reliable information. For that reason, you will find many quotes from Jefferson and Madison throughout these pages. There are no explanations from law journals in this book and you will not find any court interpretations either. The purpose of this book is to understand the principles of State sovereignty just as Americans from the original thirteen States would have when they read the Constitution and ratified it.

THE GADSDEN FLAG

DON'T TREAD ON ME!

DON'T TREAD ON ME! In other words, and in another time, its meaning was unmistakable: "Leave me alone, or else!" It was a popular phrase in the early days of America's war for independence and it is most famous for the yellow flag on which it was written just underneath a picture of a rattlesnake.

A decade prior to America's Declaration of Independence, there were several patriot groups which worked fervently for the protection of the people's individual rights. Among these were groups such as The Sons of Liberty, whose South Carolina group was led by a man named Christopher Gadsden, a Colonel who served in the Continental Army. It was Colonel Gadsden who presented this flag to Esek Hopkins, the Commander-in-Chief of America's new navy, for him to use as his personal standard. Colonel Gadsden also presented this flag to the State Legislature of South Carolina in Charleston. The record of this presentation is recorded in the South Carolina Congressional Journals:

> "Col. Gadsden presented to the Congress an elegant standard, such as is to be used by the commander in chief of the American navy; being a yellow field, with a lively representation of a rattle-snake in the middle, in the attitude of going to strike, and these words underneath, "Don't Tread on Me!"

The Gadsden flag began to gain popularity among the Americans maybe because it almost perfectly symbolized the American patriot. Before too long, this particular symbol and others like it could be seen flying over buildings or painted on signs.

In December of 1775, an anonymous letter was written to the Pennsylvania Journal in which the author signed his name as "American Guesser." There are many scholars who attribute this pen name to none other than Benjamin Franklin. This letter was written after the Revolution began but before the Declaration of Independence was signed, and it provides the reader with a unique perspective of the symbolism behind the rattlesnake.

The writer of the letter began by saying,

> "I observed on one of the drums belonging to the marines now raising, there was painted a Rattle-Snake, with this modest motto underit, 'Don't tread on me.' As I know it is the custom to have some device on the arms of every country, I supposed this may have been intended for the arms of America…I sat down to guess what could have been intended by this uncommon device…"

The writer of this letter found it appropriate that the rattlesnake be identified with the American patriot as he stated, "it occurred to me that the Rattle-Snake is found in no other quarter of the world besides America." The American patriot was constantly on guard, maintaining a keen situational awareness and therefore the rattlesnake, with its sharp eyes, "May be esteemed an emblem of vigilance." Neither the rattlesnake nor the American patriot ever strike until they have "generously given notice, even to her enemy, and cautioned him against the danger of treading on her." Another interesting point, and one that has to do entirely with the subject of this book is the opinion formed by the observant eye of the author of this letter when he stated, "I confess I was wholly at a loss what to make of the rattles, 'till I went back and counted them and found them just thirteen, exactly the number of the Colonies united in America...Tis curious and amazing to observe how distinct and independent of each other the rattles of this animal are, and yet how firmly they are united together."

The Gadsden flag is, to this day, still used by the United States Navy and it flies over America's oldest commissioned United States Naval ship, appropriately name by George Washington, the USS Constitution.

There is a patriotic awakening sweeping across America. Not since the days of the American Revolution has this symbol of liberty been the banner of a people who feel the infringements of a central government expanding by the hour. Once again, the echo of the American patriot is growing louder with every intrusive device created by the federal government. In the ears of Americans that have slumbered for too long, a rally cry is beginning to awaken them, urging them to stir themselves, and sound forth the warning: DON'T TREAD ON ME!

CHAPTER 1

"...*whenever anyone shall go about to bring them into such slavish conditions, they will always have a right to preserve what they have not a power to part with, and to rid themselves of those who invade this fundamental, sacred, and unalterable law of self-preservation,....And thus the community may be said in this respect to be always the supreme power...*"

– **John Locke**

one

THE DECLARATION OF INDEPENDENCE AND INDIVIDUAL SOVEREIGNTY

Prior to America's independence from Britain, the citizens of the British colonies in America were oppressed by a central government, a monarchy, in which sovereignty was not held by the people. That is to say inherent rights, such as freedom of speech and the ownership of private property, were not believed to be owned by the individual, but rather, they were believed to be held by the central government; the king of England. The theory that kings were endowed by God with the authority to rule, regardless of the consent of their subjects, was known as "the divine right of kings." It was through the application of this theory that the king was allowed to claim ownership over all the land in his kingdom. If you were fortunate enough, the king might grant you some land, but if he did, it was understood that the king still owned it and could recall it from your possession at any time and for any reason. The king held all sovereignty; therefore, the land always belonged to him.

Not only did the land belong to the king but the people were essentially owned by the king as well. It was the king that established what social class you would be a part of; if you were lucky enough, the king might grant you a title of nobility and a certain amount of permissions with his land and people as well. It was the king that told you what you were allowed to say, what you were not allowed to say, what religion you had to practice, what taxes you must pay and how often you would pay them. The king was not a public servant as our President is *supposed* to be. The king was simply the ruler by luck of birth, and he was sovereign over his entire kingdom and everything in it. There were instances in English history, though revolutionary and few, in which the English people declared, for specific issues, the supremacy of law over the traditional doctrine of the divine right of kings. You may remember hearing of such cases when studying documents such as the Magna Charta or The Petition of Rights in history class.

The most remarkable document to establish the principles of the rule of law came from the American colonies when the Second Continental Congress unanimously approved the Declaration of Independence to sever the political bonds which connected the colonies to British rule. The specific purpose of the Declaration of Independence was to declare the separation of the American colonies from Britain. The Founding Fathers of American government believed that the sole purpose of government was for the benefit of protecting the rights of the citizens, not the right of the rulers. They also believed that the doctrine of the divine right of kings was an oppressive, moral transgression against humanity and that no government, man, or woman for that matter, had the right to rule over his fellow man without their consent. Congress adopted the Declaration of Independence on July 4, 1776, and this date has been celebrated as the birthday of the United States of America ever since.

The Declaration of Independence is the cornerstone of our American government. Although the United States Constitution provides us with the walls of American government, those walls only stand because of the self-evident truths and principles outlined in the Declaration of Independence. For example, look at the principles that Thomas Jefferson wrote into its text where it says "We hold these Truths to be self-evident, that all Men are created equal..." Stated here is the principle of equality. The Declaration of Independence goes on to say, "That they are endowed by their Creator with certain unalienable rights." This is where Jefferson mentions inherent rights. Although we are not created with equal physical attributes, abilities, or wealth, we are created equal under God and the Law.

The Declaration of Independence is most remarkable for its revolutionary statement, "That to secure these Rights, Governments are instituted among Men." This statement boldly declares that the only valid purpose behind the existence of *any* government is to do one thing: protect individual rights. Have you ever wondered how your tax money being sent to someone who hasn't even applied for a job in the last six months does *anything* to protect your right to keep your own income? Have you ever wondered how congress could introduce over 5,000 bills a year and *all* of them be for the protection of your rights? My guess is that most of those bills, in some way or another, do nothing more than infringe on your rights, even if it's just by wasting your tax money or regulating what kind of light bulbs you are allowed to use.

Now let me quote the previous part of the Declaration of Independence and continue on just a little with the principle that defines the existence of the US Constitution and tells you what this little book is all about. This is the principle:

> "That to secure these Rights, Governments are instituted among Men, deriving their just powers from the consent of the governed."

Let me touch on the last part of that quote where it says, "deriving their just powers from the consent of the governed." It is from this that the principle of self-government is taken. From the Declaration of Independence, we can come to the conclusion that government is only legitimate if it does the following two things:

1. Secures and protects the inherent rights of the citizens
2. Operates with the consent of the citizens

One excellent way to establish your political view would be to read the Declaration of Independence and use the principles it contains as a filter of sorts. In other words, if the government, at any level, is operating without having met the criteria listed above, then it may very well be infringing on your inherent, God given, rights to one extent or another. As you read through this book, you will understand that American citizens should make a big deal out of small infringements.

In the Declaration of Independence, Thomas Jefferson wrote, "All Men are created equal, that they are endowed by their Creator with certain unalienable Rights, that among these are Life, Liberty, and the Pursuit of Happiness..." In other words, what our Founding Fathers were asserting was the fact that the King of England, or any king for that matter, did not hold all inherent rights and sovereignty unto himself. Simply because all men are created equal, all men are sovereign; each one unto himself is bestowed with sovereignty at the moment of creation and therefore, each man is his own king.

What exactly does it mean to be sovereign? I am glad you asked! If you were to pick up a Black's Law Dictionary, you would most likely find a couple of definitions similar to these:

Sovereignty – Holding supreme dominion, authority, or rule.

Sovereign – A person, body, or state bestowed with independent and supreme authority.

The easiest way to illustrate sovereignty is to give you the example of a man who owns one acre of land that borders your property. If you want to walk across his land you will have to ask his permission. He may not give you permission, but if he does, you will be allowed to walk across his land. You must ask permission only because the land you want to use does not belong to you; you have no right to it. Let's say that your neighbor gives you permission to walk across his land, but after three weeks he decides he does not want you on his property anymore so he tells you to get off and never step foot on his land again. As the owner of the property, he can do this without a reason because he is the supreme authority; he is the chief ruler, and he is sovereign. You, however, can walk across, build fences on, dig holes in, and burn *your* land if you choose to because *you* own it; *you* have the right to it. *You do not need to ask permission to exercise your right*; you are sovereign. You only need to ask permission if you don't have a right.

What you need to understand is that you are a sovereign individual. You are bestowed with the sole owner-ship of your person; therefore, you have the supreme authority over the inherent rights that God gave you at the exact moment of your creation. For example, your thoughts are inherent because your thoughts cannot be separated from your mind and you are sovereign over your thoughts because you own them; you have the supreme authority over them, and no one can take them from you or control them for you. Alexander Hamilton may not have always been the best champion of limited government, but he was right on when he explained,

> "The sacred rights of mankind are not to be rummaged for, among old parchments, or musty records. They are written, as with a sun beam in the whole volume of human nature, by the hand of the divinity itself; and can never be erased or obscured by mortal power."

Just for further understanding, you, and only you, own the rights to your body, your thoughts, as well as the right to do what is necessary to preserve your life. You have a conscience that is inherent and therefore cannot be sepa-rated from you either. You have the inherent right of self preservation just by the virtue of the laws of nature; your body's sole function is to keep you alive. Your individual and inherent rights will always be with you until the day you die simply because they cannot be extracted from your person; you are a sovereign individual.

Although inherent rights cannot be removed from us, the evening news is a constant reminder of the oppressive totalitarian governments around the world that enslave their citizens. History is littered with tyrants who claim ownership of the people, regulating their speech, their religious practices, their pursuit of happiness, etc...Although it would *appear* that sovereignty can be taken away from the individual, the truth still remains the same; all men are created equal and we are all endowed by our Creator with unalienable rights; rights that cannot be surrendered, sold or transferred to someone else.

Although inherent rights cannot by any means be extracted from you, it is possible for you to allow someone else to suppress them; at the most, you can let them claim ownership of you. For example, if you tell me that someone has taken away your freedom of speech, I will tell you that it is only because you surrendered your freedom to speak when you decided that you were *unwilling* to speak; you have allowed yourself to be enslaved. Thomas Jefferson often refers to inherent rights as "Natural Law" because your *freedom* of speech is just as *natural* as your *ability* to speak; you are using the faculties that your Creator gave you in order to manifest your inherent rights and abilities. These natural rights are yours until you die, at the most, you may choose not to exercise them; however, no one can by any means take them from you; once again, you are a sovereign person.

One of our Founding Fathers, Patrick Henry, is remembered for a speech he gave in which he declared, "Give me liberty, or give me death!" What Mr. Henry is enlightening us to is the fact that there is no middle ground between liberty and slavery. You are never only half free or only one-third a slave; you are either free or you are not. Either you claim absolute ownership over yourself, or you do not. Those men and women around the world who died fighting for their freedom did, in fact, die free. The point is this: you will always be free as long as you exercise your freedom; even if you exercise freedom in the face of opposition, you are still free. The day you surrender you freedom is the day you enslave yourself. The only other alternative to slavery is death, hence Mr. Henry's famous quote, "Give me Liberty or give me death." You are a sovereign individual no matter what. The question is this: will you fold and give yourself over to slavery or will you exercise your sovereignty even if it means death?

After several years of bloodshed, the British finally recognized America's Declaration of Independence. Soon afterward, a new government was created with the ratification of the United States Constitution. Written over the course of several months of debate, the US Constitution was composed for the purpose of establishing a government designed solely to protect the individual rights of its citizens. Our Founding Fathers established new and innovative measures to ensure that the new American government would always be in the hands of the people so that the government could only operate with the consent and particular involvement of the citizens themselves.

The United States Constitution could not be complete without establishing within it the principles of individual sovereignty and self government as written in the Declaration of Independence; and as you will see, it has. Americans, unlike the people of any other country, have a governing document designed for the protection of the individual. We have a Constitution that we can fly as a personal standard just as our forefathers flew the Gadsden flag. We have a document saturated with principles which serve as a warning to our government should it ever work against our consent or to infringe upon our inherent rights. The warning is clear: DON'T TREAD ON ME!

CHAPTER 2

"The government of the United States is a definite government, confined to specified objects. It is not like state governments, whose powers are more general."

– James Madison
Speech in the House of Representatives
January 10, 1794

two

STATE SOVEREIGNTY

What's the point of having States at all when the federal government does everything anyway? Do States even have any real power? I have heard these questions many times before but they always come from people who have not yet learned their history or their Constitution. Based on the information in this book, I would argue that the States have nearly *all* the power. I would argue that the original intent behind the US Constitution was to empower the people through their State governments and limit the power of the federal government, all in an effort to keep the American government small and unable to encroach upon the liberty of the people. I would argue that a central government, as we know it, wasn't even part of the *original* plan at all.

My arguments may sound strange to you but if you look at the Declaration of Independence, you will see that it is titled, "The unanimous Declaration of the thirteen united States of America." Notice that the "u" in "united" is not capitalized. The colonies were not declaring separation as a single sovereign entity. They were using the word "united" simply to describe that each colony had made its own decision to separate based on the principles in the Declaration. In other words, they were saying, "We're each independent, but we're in this together." In fact it would not have been uncommon to hear the delegates attending the Continental Congress and even the Constitutional Convention to refer to their home State as their "country." After the Declaration of Independence was made, each State had its own distinct form of money and many of them even maintained different forms of political organization. For all intent and purpose, they were each a separate country, some of which, history tells us, almost went to war with each other!

During the Revolutionary War, the States entered into an agreement with a document called the Articles of Confederation. The Articles of Confederation did not really serve the functions of a central government so much as it served as merely an alliance between the States as they waged a war against their common enemy, Britain. In fact you can read for yourself the intent of the Articles of Confederation; Article II and III make clear that the States were separate, sovereign, and independent. It was not until after the British surrendered that the States found out that they needed an agreement that would create a greater harmony between the States by helping to solve the problems they had with the different currencies, etc... They found the remedy in the United States Constitution, a document that created just enough of a central government for the purpose stated in the Preamble; to ensure domestic tranquility, provide for the common defense, and promote the general welfare.

You will begin to see, as you read this little book, that the US Constitution establishes nearly an indefinite scope of power to the States for them to handle separately, according to the will of the people. Although most Americans have a problem with one federal program or another, the real power over most of these programs belongs to the people at the State level. When the federal government pushes into the jurisdiction of the States, the States have the power to push back. Unfortunately for the people of the States, their legislatures are intimidated by a group of people who sit in a white building hundreds or even thousands of miles away. I often wonder how anyone can be afraid of fighting against a government full of people who are too lazy to read the bills they are voting on in the first place. I consider it a moral transgression for our States not to stand up against the encroachments of the central government! It is the duty of the States to keep that sovereignty that is guaranteed to them in the Constitution; the sovereignty that ultimately belongs to each and every one of us on an individual level.

The truth is plain: the power belongs to the people; to the States! The federal government has no Constitutional authority to regulate our daily lives! So why, then, is it that the federal government feels it has to come into our homes and tell us what kind of light bulbs we can and cannot have? Why does Washington DC feel the need to tell home owners what kind of windows we need to have? Why is it that the President and congress are involved in telling us what kind of car we can and cannot drive? Why is it that we let the federal government violate our rights with the excuse of "saving the planet?" Why is it that the States have been allowing the federal government to cross into the jurisdiction constitutionally reserved for the people of the individual States? Somebody please explain to me why the States are allowing the federal government to wrap so much red tape around every aspect of our lives at the cost of trillions of dollars that we don't even have. I want to know why the States trust the federal government with State issues when the federal government can't even be trusted with the powers that are enumerated to them in the Constitution! Yeah, that's right, the federal government can't protect our borders, it can't protect our currency, it can't be trusted with the most powerful military the world has ever known, but they want us to trust them with our healthcare!

Are you angry yet? Because I'm angry! Millions of Americans are angry, but the problem is that they do not know the US Constitution. The Constitution is our Gadsden flag, established and ordained by We the People. Pick it up; take it with you; wave it high; give it a voice! Surround the powers that be and shout until their eardrums shatter: DON'T TREAD ON ME!

CHAPTER 3

"Leave no authority existing not responsible to the people."

– Thomas Jefferson to Isaac H. Tiffany, 1816

three

THE PREAMBLE
TO THE CONSTITUTION

On May, 25, 1787, having met a quorum of seven States, the Constitutional Convention opened in Philadelphia for the purpose of revising the Articles of Confederation. James Madison however, came prepared for establishing a *new* form of government altogether. His plan was called the Virginia Plan, and it was composed of three branches of government; a legislative, executive, and judicial branch. Edmund Randolph, the Governor of Virginia, introduced the plan on the convention floor. After four months of exhaustive debate, the new Constitution was approved by all twelve State delegations, at which point it was sent to the States for ratification. In June of the following year, the United States Constitution became effective when New Hampshire became the ninth State to ratify it. After several years of revolution, the promise of the Declaration of Independence was fulfilled. America's new government completely stamped out the doctrine of the divine right of kings and replaced it with the unwavering rule of law, the United States Constitution. America was now a Constitutional Republic.

Perhaps the most remarkable part of the US Constitution is the very beginning. Before the various articles and sections are even written, the Constitution opens with a short introduction called the Preamble. Although the Preamble to the United States Constitution does not assign any powers or limitation to the federal government, it is a clear and concise introductory statement which identifies not only the Constitution's fundamental purpose but also its basic, guiding principles. The Preamble reads as follows:

> "We the People of the United States, in order to form a more perfect Union, establish Justice, insure domestic Tranquility, provide for the common defence, promote the general Welfare, and secure the Blessings of Liberty to ourselves and our Posterity, do ordain and establish this Constitution for the United States of America."

What is so extraordinary about the Preamble to the United States Constitution is that it declares, "We the People of the United States…do ordain and establish this Constitution for the United States of America," thus ensuring, with absolute clarity, that the authority for the establishment of the new government originates with the people alone. The Preamble makes it crystal clear that the government works for the people; it is the public servant of the people. The Preamble states that the government has been established by the consent of the governed and in that sense, the same principle derived from the Declaration of Independence has been applied to the Constitution.

There is an old maxim that says the creation can never rise above the creator. It makes perfect sense then that the flow of all government authority always begins with the citizens of the government. Since the Constitution was ordained and established by "We the People," then it is truth of both logic and law that "We the People" supersede the powers within it. That means that the President of the United States of America as well as every senator, congressman, governor, and every other elected official answers to the people of America. Not only does the *elected* leadership answer to the people, but the *appointed* leadership answers to the American people as well. All government employees, those employed by the government for carrying out its functions, must answer to the people. This includes everyone from the president to federal judges, to the clerks of the US Postal service; they are all government employees whose wages come from the American taxpayer.

The second phrase of the Preamble states that the Constitution was created, "to form a more perfect Union." This was the main reason for the creation of the new Constitution. The Articles of Confederation unified the States so loosely that there were many problems. Our Founding Fathers debated different thoughts time and again until they found a reasonable solution. The solution they needed was a central government with limited authority, just powerful enough to effectively handle the issues that the States could not handle on their own. We will understand these issues more as we read the chapters ahead that discuss the enumerated powers of the federal government.

The Preamble goes on to list other reasons for its establishment, such as to ensure domestic tranquility. The words "domestic tranquility" refers to the peace and cohesion between the several States. Prior to the ratification of the Constitution, each State printed and coined its own currency, making interstate commerce much more difficult, especially in the New England States which were smaller and participated in a much greater deal of interstate commerce. The new Constitution provided a means to erase the problems that often caused the States to feud with one another.

The meaning of the phrase "promote the general welfare" is a highly debated topic among many circles of students of history and government alike. Although the Preamble to the Constitution does not grant any authority to any branch of government or person, there is an argument that the words "general welfare" are meant to be used in an unlimited and literal sense. The other place where these two words are presented is in the opening section of Article 1 Section 8. When we get to that chapter, I will use the words of the Founding Fathers to discover that the words "general welfare" are to be used as nothing more than a general description for the purpose of the Constitution and the enumerated powers given to the federal government. In the 18th century, the word welfare, as used in the Constitution, meant well being; happiness; prosperity; to fare well. The federal government was created by the people to promote the "well-being" of the States.

Lastly, the Preamble mentions that the reason for the establishment of the Constitution is to secure the blessings of liberty to the people. At this point, another fundamental principle from the pages of the Declaration of Independence is applied to the intent of the Constitution in that it is designed to protect the inherent rights and liberties of the people. Having briefly discussed the Preamble, we can easily conclude that, in short, the Preamble to the United States Constitution declares that the people consent to the establishment of the government *only* to act as the protector of their rights, their inherent God given liberty and their sovereignty.

Having taken the time to read and understand the fundamental principles of the founding of American government, individual rights and sovereignty, it may now be easier to understand that the US Constitution is structured to keep the federal government small with the vast amount of sovereignty being reserved to the States and to the people. Let us now get to the heart of the matter, and delve into the Constitution itself, lifting from its text the principles of State sovereignty and self-government.

CHAPTER 4

"Whenever power may be necessary for the national government, a certain portion must be necessarily left with the states."

– James Madison, Federalist No. 62

ARTICLE 1 SECTION 3
State Sovereignty and US Senators

Although one of the most debated issues at the Constitutional Convention was the apportionment of United States Senators to the States, the principles that defined the role of the Senator were understood and agreed upon. From the text of Article 1 Section 3, prior to the ratification of the 17th Amendment, we understand that the role of Senator is designed to be a check on the federal government by the State in a sole effort by the State to maintain its Constitutional sovereignty. Here is the first part of Article 1 Section 3 prior to the ratification of the 17th amendment:

> "The Senate of the United States shall be composed of two Senators from each State, chosen by the Legislature thereof, for six years; and each Senator shall have one vote."

James Madison, the Father of the Constitution, explains the intent behind having US Senators as well as the wisdom in having them appointed by the State legislatures.

Madison believed that in order for the States to protect their rights, they must be active participants in the affairs of the federal government. Here are Madison's words:

> "Whenever power may be necessary for the national government, a certain portion must be necessarily left with the states, it is impossible for one power to pervade the extreme parts of the United States so as to carry equal justice to them. *The state legislatures also ought to have some means of defending themselves against the encroachments of the national government.* In every other department we have studiously endeavored to provide for its self-defense. Shall we leave the states alone un-provided with the means for this purpose? *And what better means can be provided than by giving them some share in, or rather make them a constituent part of, the national government?"* (Emphasis added)

Let's look at Madison's words for a moment. He said that a certain portion of federal power must be left to the hands of the States. Madison stated that it is impossible for the central government to rule over all the States and carry out its duty with equality under the law unless the States have their own means of defending themselves with representation. This makes perfect sense unless you believe that the government executes its delegated functions perfectly, and if that is what you believe, this book is above your grasp of reality.

Madison goes on to say that, "The state legislatures also ought to have some means of defending themselves against the encroachments of the national government." According to Article 1 Section 3, prior to the ratification of the 17th amendment, United States Senators were chosen by the Legislatures of the States; this provided the States with the appropriate means of defense. This method of establishing Senators by appointment would do a tremendous service for protecting the sovereignty of the individual States in more than one way. First of all, the office of United States Senator would be an appointed position made by a collective group of State legislatures, thus encouraging the Senator to fulfill his duty as a spokesperson for the leadership of the State. James Madison said the appointments of US Senators were recommended to ensure the understanding that government authority derived from the people and the States. In Federalist No. 62 Madison wrote:

> "Giving to the state governments such an agency in the formation of the federal government, as must secure the authority of the former, and may form a convenient link between the two systems."

By allowing the States to appoint their own Senators, the individual State would then have the necessary means of defending itself against the encroachments of the national government. The Constitution provides other resources for the protection of State sovereignty, but as Madison pointed out, what better means can be provided to the protection of the States than by making them an *actual mechanical part of the workings of the national government*? This would establish Senators whose duty is bound to their State and not the nation as a whole. An appointed Senator would be given the office by the elected State legislatures and sent to the federal government in Washington DC to be a check on the federal government, duty bound to represent and protect the sovereignty of his respective State from federal encroachments.

Another reason behind the appointment procedure is so that if a Senator was not representing the will and the sovereignty of his State, then the State legislature could convene and remove him from office and appoint another in his place. In other words, although US Senators served six year terms, they could be "hired and fired" if necessary in order for each State to maintain individual sovereignty. I have heard Americans voice their disappointment time and again when their Senator ignores them, refuses to hear them or represent them in Washington DC. The only solution anyone ever has to this predicament is to wait until the six-year term of the wayward Senator expires, and then vote him out of office. Our Founding Fathers had a better idea, however, when they drafted the Constitution. Before the ratification of the 17th Amendment, Senators would routinely meet with the State legislatures in order to discuss the will and the priorities of the State. This would allow the Senator to better represent the sovereignty of the State in relation to the affairs of the federal government. The Senator was in a position where he must act on behalf of his State alone and not the influence of lobbyists, friends, the president, or even a political party; he almost *had* to be a statesman. If however, the Senator chose to be a politician, he may lose his job.

Here is something else to think about: prior to the ratification of the 17th Amendment, US Senators never had to raise millions of dollars in order to campaign for an election. This eliminated all kinds of problems that pertain to temptation, corruption, making campaign promises that were never intended to be kept, as well as all the baggage that comes with the effort it takes to stay popular. The role of the United States Senator is to protect the sovereignty of his individual State so that the State legislatures can operate freely based on the will of the people that elected them. With the appointment of Senators, it would be necessary for the people to have more involvement in the State governments. Considering the original process by which US Senators were seated, attention to the election of State legislatures would be seen as more important than some see them today and thereby encourage more government participation at the State level. If we went back to appointing Senators, we would also go back to a higher level of accountability in government and leave most, if not all, of the political nonsense (scandals, campaign lies, special interest corruption) behind.

The 17th Amendment to the United States Constitution was ratified by the States on April 8th, 1913. The first sentence reads as follows:

"The Senate of the United States shall be composed of two Senators from each State, elected by the people thereof, for six years; and each Senator shall have one vote."

When the States ratified the 17th amendment to the US Constitution, a fundamental change took place that was, for the most part, completely unintended. To put it simply, the unfortunate change was the turning of Senators from statesman into politicians. With the ratification of the 17th amendment, we have allowed the duty of United States Senators to blow with the political wind away from the States and into whatever means of security they think will keep them in office. A Senator's duty can be to almost anything now; their political party, whatever demographic is going to keep them in office, the breaking of laws (such as immigration) when it appears to be popular or if it can get them extra votes. The problems with the 17th amendment have even been recognized by US Senators including one from Georgia, former US Senator Zell Miller, who stated from the floor of the Senate:

"Direct elections of Senators…allowed Washington's special interest to call the shots, whether it is filling judicial vacancies, passing laws or issuing regulations."

With the ratification of the 17th amendment, the American people have thrown the United States Senator from off the principled pedestal of statesmanship and into the arena of power politics.

The 17th amendment *must* be repealed in order for the States to reign in our Senators and bind them down to their Constitutional duty to protect the sovereignty of the individual State and thereby further the protection of individual sovereignty. It is the role of the United States Senator to stand in Washington DC as the ambassador and voice of his individual State. Our Constitution is designed so that there could be no special interest for a US Senator other than his State! The role of the United States Senator is to speak for the interest of his State, and boldly declare to the federal powers: DON'T TREAD ON ME!

CHAPTER 5

"[T]he powers of the federal government are enumerated; it can only operate in certain cases; it has legislative powers on defined and limited objects, beyond which it cannot extend its jurisdiction."

**– James Madison,
Speech in the Virginia Ratifying Convention
June 6, 1788**

five

ARTICLE 1 SECTION 8
The Enumerated Powers of the Legislative Branch

Part of understanding the restrictions of the federal government is being able to understand who exactly gets to make the federal laws. It is worth noting that the very first sentence of Article 1 Section 1 makes this very clear. Article 1 Section 1 reads as follows:

> "All legislative powers herein granted shall be vested in a Congress of the United States, which shall consist of a Senate and the House of Representatives."

As clear as this is, there still seems to be some debate as to whether or not either of the other two branches, the executive and the judicial, can legislate as well. Let me rephrase Article 1 Section 1 in a way that does not interpret it, but rather, just as simply put, leads us to the same end: *Neither the President or any member of the executive branch nor the Supreme Court or any member of the judicial branch shall exercise **any** legislative power because **all** legislative power is given to congress.* Let us now take this conclusion to the end:

*Any law or legislation that comes from anyone but congress is, from the beginning, **entirely** unconstitutional.* This would include the *legislative* actions taken by the President when he exerts a legislative signing statement or an executive order. Article 1 Section 1 also makes unconstitutional the practice of "legislating from the bench" by judges.

Now that we have established that all Constitutional legislation comes from the congress, we must, for the sake of understanding our State sovereignty, understand the limits of federal legislative authority. Such limits of authority can be found, for example, in Article 1 Section 8 of the Constitution, which gives the federal government certain powers. It is also important to note that the entire text of Article 1 Section 8 is contained in *one sentence*. I tell you this because it is absolutely paramount to understand that each one of the enumerated powers in Article 1 Section 8 is listed in the same sentence as the opening phrase and therefore all the powers given to the federal legislature must be held within the same context established at the beginning of the article. The beginning of Article 1 Section 8 reads like this:

> "The Congress shall have Power To lay and collect Taxes, Duties, Imposts and Excises, to pay the Debts and provide for the common Defence and the general Welfare of the United States;"

The context of Article 1 Section 8 is established to mean that "Congress shall have Power To" do those things listed Article 1 Section 8; to provide for the common defense and general welfare. The basis for this context is plainly stated but just to make it clearer, let's reinforces the context of congressional *powers* by contrasting them with the *limitations* placed on congress in Article 1 Section 9, which specifically states what congress cannot do. In other words, just as the powers that congress has enumerated to them are listed in Article 1 Section 8, some powers that congress does not have are listed in Article 1 Section 9.

You may take the argument that if congress has only a certain amount of powers in Article 1 Section 8 then the list of powers that they do not have would be indefinite. At this point we would have to list all powers they do not have or we would have to not list any powers they do not have, just for the sake of clarity. That is understandable but again we must keep the two sections of Article 1 in context. Article 1 Section 9 makes clear that the powers enumerated to congress have limits as well. For example, congress has the power enumerated to them "To regulate Commerce...among the several States," but Article 1 Section 9 places a limit on that power by stating that the federal government cannot tax or place a duty "on Articles exported from any State."

There are less than twenty powers enumerated to congress, so for the sake of time, let's just look at a couple of them. For example, congress has the constitutional authority and duty to provide and maintain a Navy as well as establish post offices and post roads. Let's look a bit deeper into another enumerated power given to congress and try to understand why congress is given legislative authority limited to only certain powers. The "Power To...declare War" is a power enumerated to congress and congress alone. States are pro-hibited from engaging in war, as per Article 1 Section 10, except in cases of self-defense. This is due to the fact that such actions would compromise the security and general welfare of the sister States, if not the entire country. The power is then left up to the congress at the federal level because it's a power best not left to the States for the reasons already stated.

Although the President is Commander-in-Chief of the Armed Forces of the United States, the branch of government with the Constitutional authority to declare war is the Legislative branch. The reason the power to declare war only belongs to congress is because war is a commitment that requires, maybe more than any other, the consent of the people and therefore the people must have the only voice in that commitment.

Also, it is the legislative branch of government that provides the most direct route to the will of the people. The legislative branch is designed so that it can better maintain a more pure form of representation due to how often its elected seats come up for re-election and also because there is a representative for every certain number of people. This is why it is so important for the American people to demand accountability from our elected leaders when the country is leaning toward military action. Congress alone has the constitutionally enumerated power to send our troops into war and it is unconstitutional for them to delegate that power to anyone else unless "We the People" amend the Constitution to allow for that.

At the end of Article 1 Section 8, congress is given the authority to "Make all Laws which shall be necessary and proper for carrying into Execution the foregoing Powers..." This last part of Article 1 Section 8 completes the parameter of Constitutional authority that congress has. We now understand that congress has enumerated powers over specific issues and any and all laws they pass must be identified as being necessary and proper in order to execute their enumerated powers. Congress cannot pass legislation unless it revolves, entirely, around a power that is enumerated to them. Let's just further note the previously stated maxim that the creation can never rise above the creator as a way to point out that the legislation created as necessary to the execution of an enumerated power must *always* relate only to the *direct* execution of the enumerated power, *and the new law cannot create a new power* outside of the enumerated power for which it was enacted.

According to James Madison, laws established as necessary and proper are only constitutional so long as they are confined within the jurisdiction of the enumerated powers as he explained to the Virginia Ratifying Convention on June 6th, 1788:

> "The powers of the federal government are enumerated: it can only operate in certain cases; it has legislative powers on defined and limited objects, beyond which it cannot extend its jurisdiction."

One other point of controversy seems to be the meaning of "Congress shall have Power To...provide for the...general Welfare." Some take this to mean that congress has unlimited authority to do whatever they believe to be necessary in an effort to provide for the welfare of the people. This could not be further from the truth and we will come to this conclusion, not from my own opinions, but from the thoughts of the very men who wrote these words into the Constitution. How better to understand the intent of these words than by seeking out the explanation from the authors? For example, who better to seek out for an explanation of these words than James Madison? Often called the Father of the Constitution, James Madison once elaborated on the meaning of the words "general welfare" in a letter he wrote James Robertson in which he said:

"With respect to the two words 'general welfare,' I have always regarded them as qualified by the detail of powers connected with them. To take them in a literal and unlimited sense would be a metamorphosis of the Constitution into a character which there is a host of proofs was not contemplated by its creators."

In this letter, James Madison points out that the intent behind the words "general welfare" was only to explain the reason behind enumerating any powers to the federal government at all. In other words, the government can only promote the general welfare so long as it is operates within the confines of the enumerated powers of Article 1 Section 8 of the Constitution. If the architects of the Constitution had intended to give congress unlimited power to provide for our general welfare, then what would be the point of enumerating any powers to them in the first place, since the enumerated powers would have already been covered? To use the words "general welfare" to explain powers other than those specifically enumerated would be to change the Constitution, as Madison points out, from a document used to limit the government into a document which essentially creates a government with unlimited power. A government with unlimited power is a decent description of a government that operates according to the theory of the divine right of kings, in which the king's power was unlimited.

To use the words "general welfare," as a means of providing the federal government with unlimited power, would defeat the purpose for which we separated from Britain. Thomas Jefferson clearly makes this point in a letter he wrote to Charles Hammond in 1821, read the words he used to elaborate on the character of our government as one that has limited powers. He wrote:

"When all government, domestic and foreign, in little as in great things, shall be drawn to Washington as the center of all power, it will render powerless the checks provided of one government on another and will become as venal and oppressive as the government from which we separated."

When Jefferson said, "It will render powerless the checks provided of one government on another," he is referring to the check that the State governments have on the federal government with the use of Senators. Similarly, the States cannot assume any power that has been given to the federal government and therefore, the federal government can check the States. Please note that he is not referring to the three branches of the federal government as checks on each other because they are just three branches of the *same* government; Jefferson is talking about the checks of two *different* governments on each other, the checks between the State governments and the federal government. Please remember also that the words of Madison reinforce the point that the Constitution is characterized as a limited federal government by the explicitly stated enumerated powers. The checks and balances at the federal level, as well as the checks and balances between the State governments and the federal government are designed to prevent all power from being drawn to Washington DC. Jefferson's letter tells us that an unlimited government would be just as oppressive as the government from which we fought a war to gain independence.

Our Founding Fathers understood that the Constitution was not perfect, and over time, it might be necessary to change it, to one degree or another. One concern at the time was that congress would simply legislate themselves more authority. In order to prevent congress from finding a loophole to unlimited power, the architects of the Constitution created Article 5, which governs the procedure to amend the Constitution. The Constitution was first amended with the ratification of the first ten amendments, commonly called the Bill of Rights. Thomas Jefferson pointed out the restraint on congress to this matter, as it pertains to changes that must be made to the Constitution, in a letter to Wilson Nicholas in which he said:

"Nothing is more likely than that [the] enumeration of powers is defective. This is the ordinary case of all human works. Let us then go on perfecting it by adding by way of amendments to the Constitution those powers which time and trial show are still wanting."

The Constitution is not a living document. It was not created to sit in Washington DC and constantly be reinterpreted to fit whatever or whosoever agenda it needs to fit; its principles are timeless. If government-mandated healthcare, hate crimes laws, the nationalization of banks as well as other industries, government mandates to reduce so-called "global warming" or "climate change," or government redistribution of wealth, etc… are all *so necessary*, then in order for them to be Constitutional, the Constitution *must* be amended to enumerate those powers to the federal government. We have already established that the above mentioned mandates and legislation cannot be construed to be Constitutional simply because they are done for our "general welfare." Also, they are obviously not necessary and proper in order to exercise any of the enumerated powers already defined by Article 1 Section 8. It was once said by historian Kevin Gutzman,

"Those who would give us a living Constitution are actually giving us a dead one, since such a thing is completely unable to protect us against the encroachments of government power."

The point is this: congressional legislation has jurisdiction only over the powers enumerated to them in Article 1 Section 8 of the US Constitution. Any power they create for themselves is unconstitutional, including, but certainly not limited to, government-mandated healthcare, so-called hate crimes (which is a direct violation of individual sovereignty since it puts thoughts and motivation on trial as crimes), government-mandated use of "energy efficient" light bulbs or vehicles (congress has not the enumerated power to save the planet), etc....

The People created the federal government to be our agent for certain enumerated purposes *only*. The Constitution is a contract between the people and the federal government, not to enumerate *our* power, but to enumerate the federal government's power. A Constitution that does not strictly bind down the government's authority is just what any tyrannical government would love to have, and it's what every totalitarian government *has* to have. Lord Acton was exactly right when he said, "Power corrupts, and absolute power corrupts absolutely." Any power that the federal government assumes outside the confines of the Constitution is a breach of contract and those responsible are corrupt and stand in violation of the Supreme Law of the Land, the US Constitution. If we do not understand the Constitution, how are we to know when the government is treading upon our rights? How else will we know where the lines are drawn? When will we know to sound the warning: DON'T TREAD ON ME? If you want to tell the government, DON'T TREAD ON ME! Then you *HAVE* to *KNOW* the US CONSTITUTION!

CHAPTER 6

"The great rule of conduct for us, in regard to foreign nations, is…to have with them as little political connection as possible."

– George Washington

six

ARTICLE 2 SECTION 2
US Senators and Treaties

A rticle 2 Section 2 of the Constitution provides us with the simplest proof that the United States Constitution is designed to keep the States both independent and sovereign. This article underscores and reinforces the fact that the State governments are independent and sovereign, almost as if they were each a separate country. It is this article which governs the composition of a lawful treaty of the United States of America and it reads:

> "He [the President] shall have Power, by and with the Advice and Consent of the Senate, to make Treaties, provided two thirds of the Senators present concur;"

A person who doesn't understand the reasons behind the existence of the US Senate might ask why the composition of treaties would be left up to the advice and consent of the US Senate at all. This chapter about the relation that US Senators have in conjunction with the composition of

Constitutional treaties cannot be understood until chapters one and four have been read. If you have read either chapter or both chapters one and four, you will understand, after reading the next few paragraphs, exactly why Senators are the only people who have any say in the matter of treaties at all.

Before moving forward, I think it is important to recap something we have already learned about US Senators. We learned, in chapter 4, that the sole purpose for the existence of a United States Senator is to go to Washington DC and represent the sovereignty of his State to the federal government, to be a voice for his State. The entire purpose for the very existence of the US Senator is to be involved in the affairs of the federal government so as to prevent it from encroaching upon the rights of the sovereign States.

Now that we have recapped the role of Senators, let us come to a simple understanding of what a treaty is. Black's Law Dictionary defines a treaty as: "An agreement...between two nations or sovereigns" and then goes on to point out that "Under the US Constitution, the term 'treaty' has a particular meaning—an agreement made by the President with the advice and consent of the Senate." Since a treaty is an agreement between two sovereigns, it can be said that a treaty is a compromise of the sovereignty of the parties involved so that they may find the common ground necessary for their agreement. Since the role of a Senator is to provide a voice of sovereignty for his State, it could also be said that a treaty is an agreement made by the President with the advice and consent of the *States*.

By now you may have already figured out why the Senate must be involved with the composition of treaties. By now you may begin to see that whenever the Constitution brings US Senators into a position of oversight or decision making, it is for the purpose of representing the interests of their respective State. By now you may already understand that the advice and consent of the Senate is fundamentally necessary for the declaration of a treaty by the President only because the States in the Union have a vested interest in protecting their *own* sovereignty. To put it another way, the federal government cannot compromise *national* sovereignty unless the independent States are willing to compromise *their* sovereignty.

It makes perfect sense, right? For example, the President cannot sign any treaty with the United Nations that would compromise the right of Americans to own guns *unless* the States are willing to compromise *their* independent sovereignty and allow the United Nations to come into *their* State and take firearms from *their* citizens. More national sovereignty means less international treaties; more State sovereignty means less treaties altogether. I am only using this as an example; there is plenty of evidence to prove that the US Constitution is *always* supreme and cannot be trumped by *any* treaty, especially a treaty composed contrary to the principles in the Declaration of Independence.

The words of our Founding fathers were chosen wisely, such as when Thomas Jefferson, in his first inaugural address on March 4, 1801 said, "Peace, commerce, and honest friendship with all nations, entangling alliances with none."

Many would agree that the best advice that was ever given by any of our Founding Fathers came from the one who is often referred to as the Father of America, George Washington, when he wrote in his farewell address:

"A passionate attachment of one Nation for another produces a variety of evils...against the insidious wiles of foreign influence (I conjure you to believe me, fellow-citizens) the jealousy of a free people ought to be constantly awake; since history and experience prove, that foreign influence is one of the most baneful foes of Republican Government... The great rule of conduct for us, in regard to foreign nations, is, in extending our commercial relations, to have with them as little political connection as possible. So far as we have already formed engagements, let them be fulfilled with perfect good faith. Here let us stop."

With provision after provision established to protect the sovereignty of the individual States, is this not enough evidence to prove that the Constitution is designed to keep the federal government small and the States independent and sovereign? Even after the provisions made for protecting the sovereignty of the States in Article 1 Section 3, Article 1 Section 8, and Article 2 Section 2 of the Constitution, there are still *more* provisions that provide for the protection of State sovereignty!

When the President wishes to deprive the nation and, subsequently the States, of sovereignty, it is a slippery slope. It is important for us as free people to, as George Washington said, remain jealous and constantly awake lest we lose the republic which protects our rights. We must at all times harbor the spirit of the Gadsden flag; we must always be ready to sound the warning to any nation or *United Nations*: DON'T TREAD ON ME!

CHAPTER 7

"It is of immense consequence that the States retain as complete authority as possible over their own citizens."

– Thomas Jefferson to James Monroe, 1797

seven

ARTICLE 4 SECTION 4
A Nation of Sovereign Republics

So far in this little book we have been examined the principles of individual sovereignty, and we have seen how these principles are expressed and understood in the Declaration of Independence. We have also been able to see how these principles of individual sovereignty and government with the consent of the people have shaped the US Constitution. Before the framers of the Constitution finished their work, they added another safeguard for the protection of the States. That safeguard is found in Article 4 Section 4 and it reads:

> "The United States shall guarantee to every State in this Union a Republican Form of Government..."

You may be wondering what this "guarantee" to the States means exactly. In order to understand it as it is written, we must first understand what exactly a State is and what exactly a Republic is. The word "State" is a political science word that is used to describe, basically, a community of people with a self-governing political system all of whom are located within certain territorial parameters. Black's Law Dictionary defines a State as:

> "The political system of a body of people who are politically organized; the system of rules by which jurisdiction and authority are exercised over such a body of people."

In other words, a "state" is a country that is recognized as sovereign.

Now we need to know what a government looks like when it is in Republican form. Referencing Black's Law Dictionary again, we can read the definition of a Republic as:

> "A system of government in which the people hold sovereign power and elect representatives who exercise that power."

From these two definitions, the language in Article 4 Section 4 becomes much clearer. The federal government is to guarantee that the States are governed by the will of the people and for the protection of their rights. It is important to note that the only way the people of any State can rule themselves is if they have sovereignty. In other words, each State needs its sovereignty in order to execute the functions of government that are required to protect the rights of the citizens, with the consent of the citizens. The intent of Article 4 Section 4 is consistent with the principles displayed in the Declaration of Independence. The preservation of the independent and sovereign State governments should be respected and enforced by both State and federal governments as required by the Constitution.

The Constitution clearly identifies the scope of power reserved to the State republics. Article 1 Section 8 enumerates the powers that the people have given to the federal government and Article 1 Section 9 lists some of the powers that the federal government cannot have. Article 1 Section 10 lists those things that the States cannot do but there is, however, *no enumeration of power* given to the States. Logic and reason alone are enough to justify that while the States cannot have any of the enumerated power given to the federal government or any of the powers that Article 1 Section 10 prohibits to them, *the authority over everything else falls within the jurisdiction of powers that belong to the State republics.*

The Constitution, particularly Article 4 Section 4, recognizes the right of the people to govern themselves. Understanding that the States have no enumerated powers given to them, and only a few prohibited them, the sovereignty of the individual State is not unlimited, *but it is indefinite.* That State's power is not unlimited because of some things that they cannot do. The State's power is indefinite because they are left to be the supreme authority over an indefinite amount of issues. The overwhelmingly vast majority of power is secured to the people of each independent State to be exercised in a Republican fashion. States have more power over domestic issues than the federal government, and it does not matter if each State handles the same issue completely differently; it is up to the people of each State.

CHAPTER 8

"The powers delegated by the proposed Constitution to the federal government are few and defined. Those which are to remain in the State governments are numerous and indefinite."

– James Madison, Federal No. 45
January 26, 1788

THE 9th AND 10th AMENDMENTS AND STATE SOVEREIGNTY

"I consider the foundation of the [Federal] Constitution as laid on this ground: That 'all powers not delegated to the United States, by the Constitution, nor prohibited by it to the States, are reserved to the States or to the people.' [10th Amendment] To take a single step beyond the boundaries thus specifically drawn around the powers of Congress is to take possession of a boundless field of power, no longer susceptible of any definition."

— *Thomas Jefferson, 1791*

Among the first orders of business of the First Congress was the debate over establishing a Bill of Rights. Although the Constitution had made the separation and enumeration of powers very clear, the American people and the States wanted certain rights of the people to be explicitly stated within its text. After securing America's independence from Britain, our Founding Fathers understood, better than anyone else, what freedoms a despotic and tyrannical government would attempt to take from the people.

The rights enumerated to the people in the Bill of Rights are those that are required to be exercised by the people if they are to retain their power over the government. For example, the inherent freedom of speech is one that any despotic government must take in order to control information. After all, knowledge is power; so whoever controls the dissemination of information has the power. Similar to the freedom of speech, the freedoms of assembly and religion, as well as the right to bear arms and maintain a militia are all just as necessary to the people so they always have the means of establishing themselves as the ultimate authority over the government.

Not everyone believed that the Bill of Rights was necessary. For example, Alexander Hamilton believed that the structure of the Constitution was enough to bind down the federal government. He explains that the Constitution is set up so that the people of America "surrender nothing" by delegating powers to the central government. In that sense, Hamilton was right. Any federal legislation that falls outside of the confines of the Constitutional limits of congressional power is by default unconstitutional; it is a breach of contract; it is an invasion of the sovereignty of the State or the States and the will of "We the People." In Federalist No. 84, Alexander Hamilton uses the Preamble of the Constitution to explain that a Bill of Rights is not necessary. Hamilton wrote:

> "[Our Constitution is] professedly founded upon the power of the people...Here, in strictness, the people surrender nothing; and as they retain everything they have no need of particular reservations. 'WE, THE PEOPLE of the United States, to secure the blessings of liberty to ourselves and our posterity, do establish this Constitution for the

United States of America.' Here is a clear recognition of popular rights..."

Hamilton then went on to reference several articles, sections, and clauses which did, in fact, identify the structure of the new government as one that protects the rights of the people. Hamilton's main fear was that the enumeration of certain rights would lead to the belief that those rights were the only rights of the people and that they were granted by the benevolence of the government. In the end, the will of the people and the States led to the ratification of the Bill of Rights anyway.

With one hundred proposed amendments supplied to congress by the States, James Madison initiated the debate. Of the proposed amendments, only ten were selected for ratification as the people's Bill of Rights. Two amendments chosen for ratification, the ninth and tenth, were designed to be solid reinforcements of the limited role of the federal government. These two amendments did not enumerate any rights to the people; rather, they were composed in a manner that identified the freedom of the people as indefinite and almost completely unlimited.

The Ninth Amendment to the United States Constitution was written to explain that the people have rights that go beyond what is expressed in the Bill of Rights, thus eliminating Hamilton's fear that a Bill of Rights would be identified as the entirety of the rights of the people. The Ninth Amendment states:

> "The enumeration in the Constitution, of certain rights shall not be construed to deny or disparage others retained by the people."

The Ninth Amendment gives explicit attention to the protection of liberty by preventing the federal government from reaching beyond its delegated powers. In other words, the Ninth Amendment is saying "just because we list *some* of the people's rights, it does not mean that we have listed *all* of the people's rights." It also means, "*all* the rights of the people need to be protected but here is a short list of the ones that need *special* attention." The Ninth Amendment is not a delegation of power; it is a statement of understanding. The Ninth Amendment ensures the context of the Bill of Rights as a protection of the people's liberty, not as granting the people's liberty. James Madison stated this understanding as he proposed the Bill of Rights on the House floor when he said:

> "It has been objected also against a bill of rights, that, by enumerating particular exception to the grant of power, it would disparage those rights which were not placed in that enumeration, and it might follow by implication, that those rights which were not singled out, were intended to be assigned into the hands of the general government, and were consequently insecure. This is one of the most plausible arguments I have ever heard urged against the admission of a bill of rights into this system; but, I conceive, that may be guarded against."

Just as the Ninth Amendment is written to reinforce personal liberty, the Tenth Amendment is written to reinforce the limitations of the federal government by making it clear that undelegated powers belong to the people unless given by the people to the States or the federal government. Just in case the Preamble to the Constitution wasn't clear enough; in case Article 1 Sections 3 and 8 were not made clear at all; in case Article 2 Section 2 and Article 4 Section 4 left the American people wondering whether the States or the federal government had more authority to govern the people, our Founding Fathers added one last reinforcement for State sovereignty. This last reinforcement of State sovereignty came with the ratification of the Tenth Amendment to the Constitution. The Tenth Amendment says that before congress can act, it must point to one of their enumerated powers as the source of their authority; and if they do not have that power enumerated to them, then it is a power left to the people. The Tenth Amendment states:

> "The powers not delegated to the United States by the Constitution, nor prohibited by it to the States, are reserved to the States respectively, or the people."

Let me paraphrase the Tenth Amendment for you:

> "All the powers we forgot to give the federal government *and all the powers we forgot to tell the States they don't have*...those powers then, are by default, given to the States and to the people."

Here, let me paraphrase the Tenth Amendment again:

> "If they didn't put it in the Constitution then they didn't put it in Washington!"

It was America's intent all along to keep the States free from intrusiveness that might someday come from an overbearing and tyrannical central government. Also, many people do not know that Article II of the Articles of Confederation, America's first form of government, had a similar provision which clearly stated the same point:

"Each State retains its sovereignty, freedom and independence, and every power, jurisdiction, and right, which is not by this Confederation expressly delegated to the United States, in Congress Assembled."

Much like the previous declaration in the Articles of Confederation, the Tenth Amendment to the United States Constitution defines the scope of federal power as only that power enumerated to the federal government by We the People. All power that is not enumerated to the federal government must necessarily remain with the people or the States. To further assure the American people of this limit on the federal government's ability to intervene in their lives, James Madison wrote in Federalist No. 45:

"The powers delegated to the federal government are few and defined. Those which are to remain in the state governments are numerous and indefinite. The former [federal power] will be exercised principally on external objects, as war, peace, negotiation, and foreign commerce...The powers reserved to the several States will extend to all the objects which, in the ordinary course of affairs, concern the lives, liberties and properties of the people, and the internal order, improvement, and prosperity of the State."

Should the people ever decide to enumerate any more power to the federal government, we can amend the Constitution to legally provide for that delegation of power. We have already discussed the amendment procedure which is detailed in Article 5 of the Constitution.

This is why we call it the federal government: because it is a federation of sovereign States. Governments exist on two levels in America: the defined sovereignty of the federal government and the indefinite sovereignty of the State governments. Madison referred to this when he said,

> "The powers delegated to the federal government are few and defined. Those which are to remain in the state governments are numerous and indefinite."

State Sovereignty is *not* unlimited, simply because the States have delegated *some* power to congress. States do however have *indefinite* sovereignty because of the indefinite issues that exist *outside* of those powers delegated to congress. James Madison, the Father of the Constitution and the drafter of the Bill of Rights, had this to say about the sovereignty of the States:

> "[T]he government of the United States is a definite government, confined to specified objects. It is not like the state governments, whose powers are more general."

By this point, we have come to understand that the United States Constitution is saturated with the idea of having sovereign States, free to exercise all the powers reserved to them outside of those delegated to the federal government. Not only have we found that the States have a larger array of power but we have also found out that the federal government exists *only* for the benefit of the States so that they may enjoy domestic tranquility and have provided for them a common defense. We have also discovered that the federal government, according to the Constitution prior to the ratification of the 17th Amendment, could only operate with the consent of the States. It is obvious, considering the principles outlined in the Declaration of Independence, that just as our government operates only with our consent for the protection of our rights, so does the federal government operate only with the consent of the States to protect the sovereignty of the States.

CHAPTER 9

"The Constitution is not an instrument for the government to restrain the people; it is an instrument for the people to restrain the government—lest it come to dominate our lives."

– Patrick Henry

nine

THE CHAINS OF THE CONSTITUTION

"In questions of power then, let no more be heard of confidence in man but bind him down from mischief by the chains of the Constitution."

— *Thomas Jefferson*

Of all of Americas Founding Fathers, it is reasonable to assume that we could glean the *most* wisdom from the very man who authored the Declaration of Independence, Thomas Jefferson. It was Thomas Jefferson who, in just a few days, penned a document that has shown to be one of, if not the most, remarkable documents the world has ever known. The principles found within the text of the Declaration act as the foundation for the walls of American government. In other words, the Constitution was drafted as a means to establish those principles. Truly, the Constitution fulfills the promise that the Declaration of Independence made when the people of America decided they should govern themselves. Who better to counsel us on the preservation of our freedom and our Constitution than Thomas Jefferson?

Jefferson's approach to the Constitution was very simple, and in the next few pages I encourage you to align yourself with the principles of the author of the Declaration of Independence, our third president, Thomas Jefferson.

Jefferson believed that the Constitution was easy for the American people to understand on their own. Jefferson once wrote,

> "Common sense [is] the foundation of all authorities, of the laws themselves, and of their construction."

Imagine that! Common sense in government! Common sense legislation does not require a 2,000 page bill! Common sense in the construction of our laws would do an awful lot to preserve the freedom that so many have died for. Jefferson said,

> "Laws are made for men of ordinary understanding and should, therefore be constructed by the ordinary rules of common sense. Their meaning is not to be sought for in metaphysical subtleties which may make anything mean everything or nothing at pleasure."

It amazes me that anyone would think of themselves as being too stupid to understand the laws of our government as they are written. However, it never fails; every now and then someone speaks up and tries to lecture us on the absolute necessity of letting judges interpret the Constitution for us. For some reason, people have this ridiculous notion that it is impossible to understand what the Second Amendment means until the text is interpreted for us as though it were some foreign language. The fact of the matter is that we do not need some divine-like being in a black robe, sitting behind a huge desk with a hammer in his hand, to interpret it for us. Let me validate this point by reminding you that the Constitution was sent to the States and to the people for ratification *before* the establishment of the government, including the judicial branch including any judges. So where were all the constitutional lawyers and judges to interpret the Constitution for the people during the ratification process? There were none. The people had to read it for themselves and decide if they wanted it for their new form of government. The only real help the Americans had were the Federalist Papers which James Madison, Alexander Hamilton, and John Jay wrote to *explain* how the Constitution would work to protect the people's freedom.

There is nothing hard to understand about a government with checks and balances to limit its power. If fact, in 1782, Thomas Jefferson said:

> "[The purpose of our Constitution is] to bind up the several branches of government by certain laws, which, when they transgress, their acts shall become nullities; to render a rebellion, on every infraction of their rights, on the peril that their acquiescence shall be construed into an intention to surrender those rights."

From this quote it is obvious that Jefferson had complete confidence in the American people's ability to understand the Constitution. The concept of the Constitution is simple: it exists to bind up the Government by the *Rule of Law*. Jefferson believed the Constitution to be so easy to understand that the American people would *immediately* recognize *and* rebel against even the *slightest* infraction. For example, how hard is it to understand the Second Amendment? The Second Amendment sounds simple enough to me. It states:

> "A well regulated Militia, being necessary to the security of a free State, the right of the people to keep and bear Arms, shall not be infringed."

Do you need a judge to tell you what "infringed" is *supposed* to mean? The answer is ABSOLUTELY NOT! If we needed judges to interpret words for us then judges should be writing our dictionaries! How insulting for anyone to tell me that I don't know what the law means until a judge tells me how to think! It is also not up to congress or the president to tell us what the Constitution means either. The Constitution was not established and ordained by the government so the *government* could rule the people; it was established and ordained by the people so the *people* could rule the government. So then, somebody please tell me why I am being told to take some judge's interpretation of the Constitution as the authority when the Preamble *explicitly* states that it is the *people* who are the authority.

Instead of creating new interpretations of the Constitution, how about we just *keep* its timeless principles and adhere to them? How about we stop the entire practice of *"wordsmithing"* and take Jefferson's advice:

> "On every question of construction [of the Constitution], carry ourselves back to the time when the Constitution was adopted, recollect the spirit manifested in the debates, and instead of trying what meaning may be squeezed out of the text, or invented against it, conform to the probable one in which it was passed."

WOW! What a novel thought! The next time our Supreme Court hears a case on the Second Amendment, maybe they should consider the reasons it was put into the Constitution instead of trying to invent the idea that it only applies to militias, the same militias that our government has tried to outlaw. How convenient that a government would say only militias can carry arms while at the same time trying to outlaw militias. It looks to me like an all-out effort is being made to deny the people the very freedoms that are necessary to keep the government subservient. Jefferson warned us when he said:

> "Our peculiar security is in possession of a written Constitution. Let us not make it a blank paper by construction."

Jefferson is warning us against so broadly interpreting the Constitution that it may as well be a blank piece of paper. This warning is not limited to only the Second Amendment either. Since when does "hate-crimes" legislation override my First Amendment rights? Is the government inventing the idea that freedom of speech only applies to popular speech? Are they trying to squeeze my freedom of speech so tight that all I can get out is political correctness? It sounds to me like these are just *some* examples of the infractions on my rights that Thomas Jefferson said should "render a rebellion."

Thomas Jefferson also believed that anything, no matter how attractive it might be, *had to be rejected* by congress if it was not delegated to them in Article 1 Section 8. Jefferson once stated:

> "Congress has not unlimited powers to provide for the general welfare, but only those specifically enumerated."

If you remember from chapter five, Jefferson also under-stood that the Constitution was not perfect but that the imperfections could be remedied by the people with the Amendment procedure. He said:

> "Nothing is more likely that [the] enumeration of powers is defective...Let us then go on...adding... amendments."

Jefferson understood that over time, there might arise a situation or a particular desire that would lead to the enumeration of a new power to the government. He stated the obvious process that allows for us the ability to strive for the continuous "perfection" of the Constitution, the amend-ment process of Article 5. It is Article 5 which allows We the People to provide new powers to the federal government. Take for example the 13th Amendment, which outlawed slavery in America, or the 19th Amendment, which remedied the previous error of not allowing the government to accept the votes of women. By way of note, *any* power that the federal government legislates to itself is *absolutely unconstitutional*. In fact, this is what Jefferson said about these "*laws*":

> "Whensoever the General Government assumes undelegated powers, its acts are **unauthoritative, void, and of no force.**"

Hey, big government! How's THAT for original intent?!!!!!! For too long the American people have been asleep; complacent and apathetic. While we slept, our leaders in Washington have been enslaving us with out of control debt. While we have vacationed, our elected leaders have gutted our Fourth Amendment rights. While we golfed, shopped, and socialized, we have allowed the government to become so arrogant and evil that they would brand thousands of American citizens as domestic terrorists for their political views (Google search: Missouri MIAC Report and Fusion Centers). I look at Americans today and wonder if they would fasten their own chains of slavery for a chance to win Super Bowl tickets or a trip to Disney World. It may very well be that we have been fastening our own chains of slavery for generations; the pain of regret may soon replace the healthy pulse of liberty that once flowed through our veins.

The day after Thanksgiving, "Black Friday," is the busiest shopping day of the year. On this day, many Americans buy one or several newspapers to find the best "deals" on Christmas gifts they want to purchase for their family and friends. Although the headlines are telling us that the national debt has multiplied; although the articles discuss how we are on the verge of losing our national sovereignty to the United Nations, even though the newspapers are full of stories about the deep levels of corruption in Washington and the constant decline of the American dollar, millions of Americans throw these articles out in a *frothing at the mouth* frenzy to find the best price on a large screen plasma TV. Meanwhile, back in Washington, the only thing up for sale is our freedom. Do you know what this tells Washington? It tells them, "Keep me distracted, happy, or lazy and I'll let you TREAD ON ME!"

Our freedom isn't even on sale; it's on *clearance.*

Thomas Jefferson told us what to do with our Constitution if we wish to be free. He said:

> "In questions of power then, let no more be heard of confidence in man but bind him down from mischief by the chains of the Constitution."

The Constitution is a chain created *solely* for the restraint of the government. With all the information this little book has covered, it is easy to understand that the federal government is to be limited, restricted, and kept in check, not just by the different branches, but by the States *and* the people. Our chain is the Constitution. We the People are the strength of that chain but the Constitution *needs* a voice. You can bet that the Constitution has no serious voice among our elected leadership; by calling attention to the rules that bind them down, they are calling attention to the rules that they have been breaking.

Jefferson was so right when he said that we need to bind the government leaders down from their mischief. Ever wonder what 800 billion dollars worth of mischief looks like? You probably never thought, as I never thought, that you would see the day when the mischief of our leaders would drive this country into over twenty trillion dollars worth of debt; when the mischief of our leaders would identify recently returning veterans of our wars, homeschoolers, and pro-lifers as "possible extremist threats." The mischievous ambitions that rule us from Washington DC are not new but they have grown; stronger, feeding and thriving off the apathy of the American people. The mischief of our elected leaders has been ignored for decades and there is no one to blame but We the People. Whatever the government does, to one extent or another, they do it because we let them.

When the Speaker of the House, Nancy Pelosi, was asked about the Constitutionality of the Healthcare Reform bill, her immediate response was,

"Is that a serious question?"

She then turned to some reporters and said,

"For the record, that is not a serious question."

Well guess what? It happens to be the most serious question that could possibly exist! This is the most important question that could be asked, and it *should* be answered! When out-of-control egotistical statists are attempting the largest socialist coup in American history; it should be the *only* question leaving the lips of *any* American! How treasonous and arrogant for Pelosi to blatantly acknowledge her effort to undermine the same Constitution that she took an oath to uphold. Just to keep this in perspective, let's remember that our men and women in uniform take an oath to the *same* Constitution, are issued body armor, and then sent into harm's way for less than 1/20th of the tax payer-provided salary that Pelosi gives *herself*.

Right now there is a Patriotic awakening sweeping across the land; Americans are waking up to find that their freedoms are vanishing before their eyes. It is extremely important to understand that the loss of our liberty isn't taking place solely because of the misdeeds of President Obama; it is taking place due to the misdeeds of Presidents Bush, Clinton, etc. and every elected and appointed official who holds their office as a seat of *status* instead of a seat of *service*.

It's also the fault of spineless State legislatures who cower to the federal government in spite of the unlimited sovereignty the States have reserved to them. **It is time to fill our State capitols with backbone!** It is time to supply our States with the strength to push back against the encroachments of the federal government!

If there is any hope for our Republic, it will come by the hands of courageous State legislators.

From the words of Thomas Jefferson, we understand and take encouragement in the fact that as long as our Constitution is still acknowledged as the Supreme Law of the Land, it is not too late for us to once more use it as a chain. The Constitution is a chain designed solely for the binding of our federal government; a chain that is in place to protect the sovereignty of the people and the States; a chain that keeps the intrusive arm of the federal government out of the lives and homes of the citizens. As Jefferson advises us, we must remain watchful if we wish to rally and recall people to that chain, give it strength, and keep the mischief of government from growing into the tyrannical despotic government that it, by natural progress, is sure to become. A final word from Jefferson is this:

> "Though written constitutions may be violated in
> moments of passion or delusion, yet they furnish
> a text to which those who are watchful may again
> rally and recall the people."

The Constitution is our Gadsden flag, established and ordained by We the People. Pick it up; take it with you; wave it high; give it a voice! Surround the powers that be and shout until their eardrums shatter: DON'T TREAD ON ME!

CHAPTER 10

ORIGINAL INTENT
The Thoughts of Our Founding Fathers

ten

ORIGINAL INTENT
VALUABLE QUOTES FROM OUR
FOUNDING FATHERS

Valuable Quotes from the Author of the Declaration
of Independence, Thomas Jefferson and the Father
of the Constitution, James Madision

Thomas Jefferson

❖ *"I am persuaded no Constitution was ever before so well calculated as ours for extensive empire and self-government."*
   – Thomas Jefferson to James Madison, 1809

❖ *"The authority of [the] people [is] a necessary foundation for a constitution."*
   – Thomas Jefferson to John Hampden Pleasants, 1824

❖ *"I consider the foundation of the [Federal] Constitution as laid on this ground: That "all powers not delegated to the United States, by the Constitution, nor prohibited by it to the States, are reserved to the States or to the people." [10th Amendment] To take a single step beyond the boundaries thus specifically drawn around the powers of Congress is to take possession of a boundless field of power, no longer susceptible of any definition."*
– Thomas Jefferson: Opinion on National Bank, 1791

❖ *"I was in Europe when the Constitution was planned, and never saw it till after it was established. On receiving it, I wrote strongly to Mr. Madison, urging the want of provision for...an express reservation to the States of all rights not specifically granted to the Union."*
– Thomas Jefferson to Joseph Priestley, 1802

❖ *"Whensoever the General Government assumes undelegated powers, its acts are unauthoritative, void, and of no force."*
– Thomas Jefferson: Draft Kentucky Resolutions, 1798

❖ *"[An] act of the Congress of the United States...which assumes powers...not delegated by the Constitution, is not law, but is altogether void and of no force."*
– Thomas Jefferson: Draft Kentucky Resolutions, 1798

❖ *"To keep in all things within the pale of our constitutional powers...[is one of] the landmarks by which we are to guide ourselves in all our proceedings."*
– Thomas Jefferson: 2nd Annual Message, 1802

❖ *"The legitimate powers of government extend to such acts only as are injurious to others."*
– Thomas Jefferson: Notes on Virginia, 1782

❖ *"Leave no authority existing not responsible to the people."*
– Thomas Jefferson to Isaac H. Tiffany, 1816

❖ *"Our country is too large to have all its affairs directed by a single government. Public servants at such a distance, and from under the eye of their constituents, must, from the circumstance of distance, be unable to administer and over-look all the details necessary for the good government of the citizens; and the same circumstance, by rendering detection impossible to their constituents, will invite public agents to corruption, plunder and waste."*
– Thomas Jefferson to Gideon Granger, 1800

❖ *"I believe the States can best govern our home concerns, and the General Government our foreign ones."*
– Thomas Jefferson to William Johnson, 1823

❖ *"They are not to do anything they please to provide for the general welfare...[G]iving a distinct and independent power to do any act they please which may be good for the Union, would render all the preceding and subsequent enumerations of power completely useless. It would reduce the whole instrument to a single phrase, that of instituting a Congress with power to do whatever would be for the good of the United States; and as they sole judges of the good or evil, it would be also a power to do whatever evil they please."*
– Thomas Jefferson

❖ *"My general plan would be, to make the States one as to everything connected with foreign nations, and several as to everything purely domestic."*
– Thomas Jefferson to Edward Carrington, 1787

❖ *"The States supposed that by their tenth amendment, they had secured themselves against constructive powers."*
– Thomas Jefferson to William Johnson, 1823

❖ *"The States should be left to do whatever acts they can do as well as the General Government."*
– Thomas Jefferson to John Harvie, 1790

❖ *"It is of immense consequence that the States retain as complete authority as possible over their own citizens."*
– Thomas Jefferson to James Monroe, 1797

❖ *"The several States composing the United States of America are not united on the principle of unlimited submission to their General Government; but...by a compact under the style and title of a Constitution for the United States, and of amendments thereto, they constituted a General Government for special purposes—delegated to that government certain definite powers, reserving, each State to itself, the residuary mass of right to their own self-government."*
– Thomas Jefferson: Draft Kentucky Resolutions, 1798

❖ *"It is a fatal heresy to suppose that either our State governments are superior to the Federal or the Federal to the States. The people, to whom all authority belongs, have divided the powers of government into two distinct departments, the leading characters of which are foreign and domestic; and they have appointed for each a distinct set of functionaries. These they have made coordinate, checking and balancing each other like the three cardinal departments in the individual States; each equally supreme as to the powers delegated to itself, and neither authorized ultimately to decide what belongs to itself or to its coparcener in government. As independent, in fact, as different nations."*

– Thomas Jefferson to Spencer Roane, 1821

❖ *"The true barriers of our liberty in this country are our State governments; and the wisest conservative power ever contrived by man is that of which our Revolution and present government found us possessed."*

– Thomas Jefferson to A. L. C. Destutt de Tracy, 1811

❖ *"It is a singular phenomenon that while our State governments are the very best in the world, without exception or comparison, our General Government has, in the rapid course of nine or ten years, become more arbitrary and has swallowed more of the public liberty than even that of England."*

– Thomas Jefferson to John Taylor, 1798

James Madison

❖ *"The government of the United States is a definite government, confined to specified objects. It is not like state governments, whose powers are more general. Charity is no part of the legislative duty of the government."*

— James Madison, Speech in the House of Representative January 10, 1794

❖ *"It has been objected also against a bill of rights, that, by enumerating particular exceptions to the grant of power, it would disparage those rights which were not placed in that enumeration, and it might follow by implication, that those rights which were not singled out, were intended to be assigned into the hands of the general government, and were consequently insecure. This is one of the most plausible arguments I have ever heard urged against the admission of a bill of rights into this system; but, I conceive, that may be guarded against. I have attempted it, as gentlemen may see by turning to the last clause of the 4th resolution."*

— James Madison, Proposing Bill of Rights to House June 8, 1789

❖ *"[T]he powers of the federal government are enumerated; it can only operate in certain cases; it has legislative powers on defined and limited objects, beyond which it cannot extend its jurisdiction."*

— James Madison, Speech at the Virginia Ratifying Convention, June 6, 1788

❖ *"It is sufficiently obvious, that persons and property are the two great subjects on which Governments are to act; and that the rights of persons, and the rights of property, are the objects, for the protection of which Government was instituted. These rights cannot be separated."*

– James Madison, Speech at the Virginia Convention December 2, 1829

❖ *"If Congress can do whatever in their discretion can be done by money, and will promote the general welfare, the government is no longer a limited one possessing enumerated powers, but an indefinite one subject to particular exceptions." James Madison, "Letter to Edmund Pendleton,"*

– James Madison in a letter to Edmund Pendleton

❖ *"Government is instituted to protect property of every sort; as well that which lies in the various rights of individuals, as that which the term particularly expresses. This being the end of government, which impartially secures to every man, whatever is his own."*

– James Madison, National Gazette, March 1792
The Papers of James Madison, vol. 14 ed. R.A. Rutland (Chicago: University of Chicago Press, 1976), p. 266

❖ *"The powers delegated by the proposed Constitution to the federal government are few and defined. Those which are to remain in the State governments are numerous and indefinite."*

– James Madison, Federal No. 45, January 26, 1788

❖ *"Resolved, That the General Assembly of Virginia, doth unequivocally express a firm resolution to maintain and defend the Constitution of the United States, and the Constitution of this State, against every aggression either foreign or domestic... That this Assembly doth explicitly and peremptorily declare, that it views the powers of the federal government, as resulting from the compact, to which the states are parties; as limited by the plain sense and intention of the instrument constituting the compact; as no further valid than they are authorized by the grants enumerated in that compact; and that in case of deliberate, palpable, and dangerous exercise of other powers, not granted by the said compact, the states who are parties thereto, have the right, and are in duty bound, to interpose for arresting the progress of the evil, and for maintaining within their respective limits, the authorities, rights and liberties appertaining to them."*

– James Madison, 1799

❖ *"All men having power ought to be distrusted to a certain degree."*

– James Madison in <u>The Federalist</u>

❖ *"There are more instances of the abridgment of the freedom of the people by gradual and silent encroachments of those in power than by violent and sudden usurpations."*

– James Madison, Speech at the Virginia Ratifying Convention, June 16, 1788

❖ *"With respect to the two words "general welfare," I have always regarded them as qualified by the detail of powers connected with them. To take them in a literal and unlimited sense would be a metamorphosis of the Constitution into a character which there is a host of proofs was not contemplated by its creators. If the words obtained so readily a place in the "Articles of Confederation," and received so little notice in their admission into the present Constitution, and retained for so long a time a silent place in both, the fairest explanation is, that the words, in the alternative of meaning nothing or meaning everything, had the former meaning taken for granted."*

– James Madison in a letter to James Robertson

❖ *"I cannot undertake to lay my finger on that article of the Constitution which granted a right to Congress of expending, on objects of benevolence, the money of their constituents."*

– James Madison, in 1794 when Congress appropriated $15,000 for the relief of French refugees living in Baltimore and Philadelphia

❖ *"As a man is said to have a right to his property, he may be equally said to have a property in his rights. Where an excess of power prevails, property of no sort is duly respected. No man is safe in his opinions, his person, his faculties, or his possessions."*

– James Madison, National Gazette essay, March 27, 1792

❖ *"It will be of little avail to the people that the laws are made by men of their own choice, if the laws be so voluminous that they cannot be read, or so incoherent that they cannot be understood; if they be repealed or revised before they are promulgated, or undergo such incessant changes that no man who knows what the law is today can guess what is will be tomorrow."*

– James Madison, Federalist no. 62, February 27, 1788

❖ *"If Congress can do whatever in their discretion can be done by money, and will promote the General Welfare, the Government is no longer a limited one, possessing enumerated powers, but an indefinite one..."*

– James Madison, letter to Edmund Pendleton January 21, 1792

❖ *"Charity is no part of the legislative duty of the government."*
– James Madison

More Good Quotes

America / Americans

❖ *"Posterity—you will never know how much it has cost my generation to preserve your freedom. I hope you will make good use of it."*
  – John Adams

❖ *"I cannot be emphasized too strongly or too often that this great nation was founded, not by religionists, but by Christians; not on religions, but on the gospel of Jesus Christ. For this very reason peoples of other faiths have been afforded asylum, prosperity, and freedom of worship."*
  – Patrick Henry

❖ *"I think we have more machinery of government than is necessary, too many parasites living on the labor of the industrious."*
  – Thomas Jefferson

Constitution

❖ *"Our Constitution was made only for moral and religious people. It is wholly inadequate to the government of any other."*
  – John Adams

❖ *"Hold on, my friends, to the Constitution and to the Republic for which it stands. Miracles do not cluster and what has happened once in 6,000 years, may not happen again. Hold on to the Constitution, for if the American Constitution should fail, there will be anarchy throughout the world."*
  – Daniel Webster

❖ *"The Constitution is not an instrument for the government to restrain the people, it is an instrument for the people to restrain the government - lest it come to dominate our lives."*
– Patrick Henry

Freedom

❖ *"Resistance to tyrants is obedience to God."*
– Thomas Jefferson

❖ *"There are more instances of the abridgment of the freedom of the people by gradual and silent encroachments of those in power than by violent and sudden usurpations."*
– **James Madison**

❖ *"They who give up essential liberty to obtain a little temporary safety deserve neither liberty nor safety."*
– Benjamin Franklin

❖ *"Those who expect to reap the blessings of freedom must, like men, undergo the fatigue of supporting it."*
– Thomas Paine

Law

❖ *"We should never create by law what can be accomplished by morality."*
– Montesquieu

❖ *"When the state is most corrupt, then the laws are most multiplied."*
– Tacitus

❖ *"Where law ends, tyranny begins."*
    – William Pitt

Liberty

❖ *"Guard with jealous attention the public liberty. Suspect everyone who approaches the jewel. Unfortunately, nothing will preserve it but downright force. Whenever you give up that force, you are inevitably ruined."*
    – Patrick Henry

❖ *"God grants liberty only to those who love it and are always ready to guard and defend it."*
    – Daniel Webster

❖ *"He that would make his own liberty secure must guard even his enemy from oppression."*
    – Thomas Paine

❖ *"The liberties of a people never were, nor ever will be, secure, when the transactions of their rulers may be concealed from them."*
    – Patrick Henry

❖ *"A general dissolution of principles and manners will more surely overthrow the liberties of America than the whole force of the common enemy. While the people are virtuous they cannot be subdued; but when once they lose their virtue then will be ready to surrender their liberties to the first external or internal invader."*
    – Samuel Adams

❖ *"Liberty exists in proportion to wholesome restraint; the more restraint on others to keep off from us, the more liberty we have."*
– Daniel Webster

❖ *"Guard with jealous attention the public liberty. Suspect everyone who approaches that jewel. Unfortunately, nothing will preserve it but downright force. Whenever you give up that force, you are inevitably ruined."*
– Patrick Henry

❖ *"Those who expect to reap the blessings of freedom must, like men, undergo the fatigue of supporting it."*
– Thomas Paine

❖ *"He that would make his own liberty secure must guard even his own enemy from oppression."*
– Thomas Paine

❖ *"God grants liberty only to those who love it, and are always ready to guard and defend it."*
– Daniel Webster

❖ *"The natural progress of things is for liberty to yield and government to gain."*
– Thomas Jefferson

❖ *"The God who gave us life gave us liberty at the same time."*
– Thomas Jefferson

❖ *"Statesmen my dear Sir, may plan and speculate for Liberty, but it is Religion and Morality alone, which can establish the Principles upon which Freedom can securely stand."*
– John Adams

Patriotism

❖ *"The duty of a patriot is to protect his country from its government."*
– Thomas Paine

❖ *"These are the times that try men's souls. The summer soldier and the sunshine patriot will in this crisis shrink from the service of their country, but he that stands it now deserves the love and thanks of man and woman."*
– Thomas Paine

Government

❖ *"Civil laws are not to provide for the truth of opinion but for the safety and security of the commonwealth, and of every particular man's goods and person. And so it ought to be, for truth certainly will do well enough if she were once left to shift for herself."*
– John Locke

❖ *"The powers delegated by the proposed Constitution to the federal government are few and defined. Those which are to remain in the State governments are numerous and indefinite. The former will be exercised principally on external*

objects, as war, peace, negotiation and foreign commerce...
The powers reserved to the several States will extend to all
the objects which in the ordinary course of affairs, concern
the lives and liberties, and properties of the people, and the
internal order, improvement and prosperity of the State."
– James Madison

❖ *"We are all agents of the same supreme power, the people."*
– Daniel Webster

❖ *"Knowledge will forever govern ignorance, and a people who
mean to be their own governors, must arm themselves with
the power knowledge gives."*
– James Madison

❖ *"History, I believe, furnishes no example of a priest-ridden people
maintaining a free civil government. This marks the lowest
grade of ignorance of which their civil as well as religious leaders
will always avail themselves for their own purposes."*
– Thomas Jefferson

❖ *"thing is clear: The Founding Fathers never intended a nation
where citizens would pay nearly half of everything they earn
to the government."*
– Ron Paul

❖ *"I predict future happiness for Americans, if they can prevent
the government from wasting the labors of the people under
the pretense of taking care of them."*
– Thomas Jefferson

❖ *"Civil government, so far as it is instituted for the security of property, is in reality instituted for the defense of the rich against the poor, or of those who have some property against those who have none at all."*

– Adam Smith

❖ *"A nation can survive its fools, and even the ambitious. But it cannot survive treason from within. An enemy at the gates is less formidable, for he is known and carries his banner openly. But the traitor moves amongst those within the gate freely, his sly whispers rustling through all the alleys, heard in the very halls of government itself. For the traitor appears not a traitor; he speaks in accents familiar to his victims, and he wears their face and their arguments, he appeals to the baseness that lies deep in the hearts of all men. He rots the soul of a nation, he works secretly and unknown in the night to undermine the pillars of the city, he infects the body politic so that it can no longer resist. A murderer is less to fear."*

– Cicero

❖ *"If the people who make the decisions are the people who will also bear the consequences of those decisions, perhaps better decisions will result."*

– John Adams

❖ *"Freedom is living without government coercion. So when a politician talks about freedom for this group or that, ask yourself whether he is advocating more government action or less."*

– Ron Paul

❖ *"A wise and frugal government, which shall leave men free to regulate their own pursuits of industry and improvement, and shall not take from the mouth of labor and bread it has earned — this is the sum of good government."*
– Thomas Jefferson

❖ *"There are men in all ages who mean to govern well, but they mean to govern. They promise to be good masters, but they mean to be masters."*
– Daniel Webster

❖ *"If ever a time should come, when vain and aspiring men shall possess the highest seats in Government, our country will stand in need of its experienced patriots to prevent its ruin."*
– Samuel Adams

❖ *"Experience has shown, that even under the best forms of government those entrusted with power have, in time, and by slow operations, perverted it into tyranny."*
– Thomas Jefferson

❖ *"The spirit of resistance to government is so valuable on certain occasions, that I wish it to be always kept alive."*
– Thomas Jefferson

❖ *"There is danger from all men. The only maxim of a free government ought to be to trust no man living with power to endanger the public liberty."*
– John Adams

❖ *"Government, even in its best state, is but a necessary evil; in its worst state, an intolerable one."*
– Thomas Paine

❖ *"There is no nation on earth powerful enough to accomplish our overthrow. Our destruction, should it come at all, will be from another quarter. From the inattention of the people to the concerns of their government, from their carelessness and negligence."*
– Daniel Webster

❖ *"The policy of the American government is to leave its citizens free, neither restraining them nor aiding them in their pursuits."*
– Thomas Jefferson

❖ *"The deterioration of every government begins with the decay of the principles on which it was founded."*
– Montesquieu

❖ *"The purpose of government is to enable the people of a nation to live in safety and happiness. Government exists for the interests of the governed, not for the governors."*
– Thomas Jefferson

❖ *"I know no safe depository of the ultimate powers of the society but the people themselves; and if we think them not enlightened enough to exercise their control with a wholesome discretion, the remedy is not to take it from them but to inform their discretion by education. This is the true corrective of abuses of Constitutional power."*
– Thomas Jefferson

❖ *"Government is not reason, it is not eloquence—it is force. Like fire, it is a dangerous servant and fearful master."*
– George Washington

❖ *"I am for doing good to the poor, but...I think the best way of doing good to the poor, is not making them easy in poverty, but leading or driving them out of it. I observed...that the more public provisions were made for the poor, the less they provided for themselves, and of course became poorer. And, on the contrary, the less was done for them, the more they did for themselves, and became richer."*
– Benjamin Franklin

❖ *"If men were angels, no government would be necessary. If angels were to govern men, neither external nor internal controls on government would be necessary. In framing a government which is to be administered by men over men, the great difficulty lies in this: you must first enable the government to control the governed; and in the next place oblige it to control itself. A dependence on the people is, no doubt, the primary control on the government; but experience has taught mankind the necessity of auxiliary precautions."*
– James Madison

❖ *"My reading of history convinces me that most bad government results from too much government."*
– Thomas Jefferson

❖ *"The will of the people is the only legitimate foundation of any government, and to protect its free expression should be our first object."*
– Thomas Jefferson

Guns / Gun Control

❖ *"Before a standing army can rule the people must be disarmed; as they are in almost every kingdom in Europe. The supreme power in America cannot enforce unjust laws by the sword; because the whole body of the people are armed and constitute a force superior to any band of regular troops that can be, on any pretence, raised in the United States."*

– Noah Webster

❖ *"And that the said Constitution be never construed to authorize Congress...to prevent the people of the United States, who are peaceable citizens, from keeping their own arms..."*

– Samuel Adams

❖ *"No free man shall ever be de-barred the use of arms. The strongest reason for the people to retain their right to keep and bear arms is as a last resort to protect themselves against tyranny in government."*

– Thomas Jefferson

❖ *"A government that does not trust its law abiding citizens to keep and bear arms is itself unworthy of trust."*

– James Madison

Politics / Politician

❖ *"When a man assumes a public trust, he should consider himself as public property."*

– Thomas Jefferson

Socialism

❖ *"The utopian schemes of leveling [re-distribution of the wealth!] and a community of goods [central ownership of the means of production and distribution], are as visionary and impractical as those which vest all property in the Crown. [These ideas] are arbitrary, despotic, and, in our government, unconstitutional."*
– Samuel Adams

Statesmanship

❖ *"The great difference between the real statesman and the pretender is, that the one sees into the future, while the other regards only the present; the one lives by today, the other acts on enduring principles and for immorality."*
– Edmund Burke

Taxes

❖ *"To compel a man to furnish contributions of money for the propagation of opinions which he disbelieves and abhors, is sinful and tyrannical."*
–Thomas Jefferson

THE DECLARATION OF INDEPENDENCE

In CONGRESS – July 4, 1776

The unanimous Declaration of the thirteen United States of America

When, in the course of human events, it becomes necessary for one people to dissolve the political bonds which have connected them with another, and to assume among the powers of the earth, the separate and equal station to which the laws of nature and of nature's God entitle them, a decent respect to the opinions of mankind requires that they should declare the causes which impel them to the separation.

We hold these truths to be self-evident, that all men are created equal, that they are endowed by their Creator with certain unalienable rights, that among these are life, liberty and the pursuit of happiness. That to secure these rights, governments are instituted among men, deriving their just powers from the consent of the governed. That whenever any form of government becomes destructive to these ends, it is the right of the people to alter or to abolish it, and to institute new government, laying its foundation on such principles and organizing its powers in such form, as to them shall seem most likely to effect their safety and happiness. Prudence, indeed, will dictate that governments long established should not be changed for light and transient causes; and accordingly all experience hath shown that mankind are more disposed to suffer, while evils are sufferable, than to right themselves by abolishing the forms to which they are accustomed. But when a long train of abuses and usurpations, pursuing invariably the same object evinces a design to reduce them under absolute despotism, it is their right, it is their duty, to throw off such government, and to provide new guards for their future security. –Such has been the patient sufferance of these colonies; and such is now the necessity which constrains them to alter their former systems of government. The history of the present King of Great Britain is a history of repeated injuries and usurpations, all having in direct object the establishment of an absolute tyranny over these states. To prove this, let facts be submitted to a candid world.

He has refused his assent to laws, the most wholesome and necessary for the public good.

He has forbidden his governors to pass laws of immediate and pressing importance, unless suspended in their operation till his assent should be obtained; and when so suspended, he has utterly neglected to attend to them.

He has refused to pass other laws for the accommodation of large districts of people, unless those people would relinquish the right of representation in the legislature, a right inestimable to them and formidable to tyrants only.

He has called together legislative bodies at places unusual, uncomfortable, and distant from the depository of their public records, for the sole purpose of fatiguing them into compliance with his measures.

He has dissolved representative houses repeatedly, for opposing with manly firmness his invasions on the rights of the people.

He has refused for a long time, after such dissolutions, to cause others to be elected; whereby the legislative powers, incapable of annihilation, have returned to the people at large for their exercise; the state remaining in the meantime exposed to all the dangers of invasion from without, and convulsions within.

He has endeavored to prevent the population of these states; for that purpose obstructing the laws for naturalization of foreigners; refusing to pass others to encourage their migration hither, and raising the conditions of new appropriations of lands.

He has obstructed the administration of justice, by refusing his assent to laws for establishing judiciary powers.

He has made judges dependent on his will alone, for the tenure of their offices, and the amount and payment of their salaries.

He has erected a multitude of new offices, and sent hither swarms of officers to harass our people, and eat out their substance.

He has kept among us, in times of peace, standing armies without the consent of our legislature.

He has affected to render the military independent of and superior to civil power.

He has combined with others to subject us to a jurisdiction foreign to our constitution, and unacknowledged by our laws; giving his assent to their acts of pretended legislation:

For quartering large bodies of armed troops among us:

For protecting them, by mock trial, from punishment for any murders which they should commit on the inhabitants of these states:

For cutting off our trade with all parts of the world:

For imposing taxes on us without our consent:

For depriving us in many cases, of the benefits of trial by jury:

For transporting us beyond seas to be tried for pretended offenses:

For abolishing the free system of English laws in a neighboring province, establishing therein an arbitrary government, and enlarging its boundaries so as to render it at once an example and fit instrument for introducing the same absolute rule in these colonies:

For taking away our charters, abolishing our most valuable laws, and altering fundamentally the forms of our governments:

For suspending our own legislatures, and declaring themselves invested with power to legislate for us in all cases whatsoever.

He has abdicated government here, by declaring us out of his protection and waging war against us.

He has plundered our seas, ravaged our coasts, burned our towns, and destroyed the lives of our people.

He is at this time transporting large armies of foreign mercenaries to complete the works of death, desolation and tyranny, already begun with circumstances of cruelty and perfidy scarcely paralleled in the most barbarous ages, and totally unworthy the head of a civilized nation.

He has constrained our fellow citizens taken captive on the high seas to bear arms against their country, to become the executioners of their friends and brethren, or to fall themselves by their hands.

He has excited domestic insurrections amongst us, and has endeavored to bring on the inhabitants of our frontiers, the merciless Indian savages, whose known rule of warfare, is undistinguished destruction of all ages, sexes and conditions.

In every stage of these oppressions we have petitioned for redress in the most humble terms: our repeated petitions have been answered only by repeated injury. A prince, whose character is thus marked by every act which may define a tyrant, is unfit to be the ruler of a free people.

Nor have we been wanting in attention to our British brethren. We have warned them from time to time of attempts by their legislature to extend an unwarrantable jurisdiction over us. We have reminded them of the circumstances of our emigration and settlement here. We have appealed to their native justice and magnanimity, and we have conjured them by the ties of our common kindred to disavow these usurpations, which, would inevitably interrupt our connections and correspondence. They too have been deaf to the voice of justice and of consanguinity. We must, therefore, acquiesce in the necessity, which denounces our separation, and hold them, as we hold the rest of mankind, enemies in war, in peace friends.

We, therefore, the representatives of the United States of America, in General Congress, assembled, appealing to the Supreme Judge of the world for the rectitude of our intentions, do, in the name, and by the authority of the good people of these colonies, solemnly publish and declare, that these united colonies are, and of right ought to be free and independent states; that they are absolved from all allegiance to the British Crown, and that all political connection between them and the state of Great Britain, is and ought to be totally dissolved; and that as free and independent states, they have full power to levy war, conclude peace, contract alliances, establish commerce, and to do all other acts and things which independent states may of right do. And for the support of this declaration, with a firm reliance on the protection of Divine Providence, we mutually pledge to each other our lives, our fortunes and our sacred honor.

SIGNERS OF THE UNANIMOUS DECLARATION

John Hancock (Massachusetts)

Pennsylvania
Robert Morris
Benjamin Rush
Benjamin Franklin
John Morton
George Clymer
James Smith
George Taylor
James Wilson
George Ross

Massachusetts
Samuel Adams
John Adams
Robert Treat Paine
Elbridge Gerry

Delaware
George Read
Caesar Rodney
Thomas McKean

Connecticut
Roger Sherman
Samuel Huntington
William Williams
Oliver Wolcott

Virginia
George Wythe
Richard Henry Lee
Thomas Jefferson
Benjamin Harrison
Thomas Nelson, Jr.
Francis Lightfoot Lee
Carter Braxton

North Carolina
William Hooper
Joseph Hewes
John Penn

New Hampshire
Josiah Bartlett
William Whipple
Matthew Thornton

Maryland
Samuel Chase
William Paca
Thomas Stone
Charles Carroll
of Carrollton

New Jersey
Richard Stockton
John Witherspoon
Francis Hopkinson
John Hart
Abraham Clark

Rhode Island
Stephen Hopkins
William Ellery

South Carolina
Edward Rutledge
Thomas Heyward, Jr.
Thomas Lynch, Jr.
Arthur Middleton

Georgia
Button Gwinnett
Lyman Hall
George Walton

New York
William Floyd
Philip Livingston
Francis Lewis
Lewis Morris

THE CONSTITUTION OF THE UNITED STATES

We the People of the United States, in Order to form a more perfect Union, establish Justice, insure domestic Tranquility, provide for the common defence, promote the general Welfare, and secure the Blessings of Liberty to ourselves and our Posterity, do ordain and establish this Constitution for the United States of America.

Article I

Section 1. All legislative Powers herein granted shall be vested in a Congress of the United States, which shall consist of a Senate and House of Representatives.

Section 2. The House of Representatives shall be composed of Members chosen every second Year by the People of the several States, and the Electors in each State shall have the Qualifications requisite for Electors of the most numerous Branch of the State Legislature.

No Person shall be a Representative who shall not have attained to the age of twenty five Years, and been seven Years a Citizen of the United States, and who shall not, when elected, be an Inhabitant of that State in which he shall be chosen.

Representatives and direct Taxes shall be apportioned among the several States which may be included within this Union, according to their respective Numbers, which shall be determined by adding to the whole Number of free Persons, including those bound to Service for a Term of Years, and excluding Indians not taxed, three fifths of all other Persons. The actual Enumeration shall be made within three Years after the first Meeting of the Congress of the United States, and within every subsequent Term of ten Years, in such Manner as they shall by Law direct. The Number of Representatives shall not exceed one for every thirty Thousand, but each State shall have at Least one Representative; and until such enumeration shall be made, the State of New Hampshire shall be entitled to chuse three, Massachusetts eight, Rhode-Island and Providence Plantations one, Connecticut five, New-York six, New Jersey four, Pennsylvania eight, Delaware one, Maryland six, Virginia ten, North Carolina five, South Carolina five, and Georgia three.

When vacancies happen in the Representation from any State, the Executive Authority thereof shall issue Writs of Election to fill such Vacancies.

The House of Representatives shall chuse their Speaker and other Officers; and shall have the sole Power of Impeachment.

Section 3. The Senate of the United States shall be composed of two Senators from each State, chosen by the Legislature thereof, for six Years; and each Senator shall have one Vote.

Immediately after they shall be assembled in Consequence of the first Election, they shall be divided as equally as may be into three Classes. The Seats of the Senators of the first Class shall be vacated at the Expiration of the second Year, of the second Class at the Expiration of the fourth Year, and the third Class at the Expiration of the sixth Year, so that one third may be chosen every second Year; and if Vacancies happen by Resignation, or otherwise, during the Recess of the Legislature of any State, the Executive thereof may make temporary Appointments until the next Meeting of the Legislature, which shall then fill such Vacancies.

No Person shall be a Senator who shall not have attained to the Age of thirty Years, and been nine Years a Citizen of the United States and who shall not, when elected, be an Inhabitant of that State for which he shall be chosen.

The Vice President of the United States shall be President of the Senate, but shall have no Vote, unless they be equally divided.

The Senate shall chuse their other Officers, and also a President pro tempore, in the Absence of the Vice President, or when he shall exercise the Office of President of the United States.

The Senate shall have the sole Power to try all Impeachments. When sitting for that Purpose, they shall be on Oath or Affirmation. When the President of the United States is tried, the Chief Justice shall preside: And no Person shall be convicted without the Concurrence of two thirds of the Members present.

Judgment in Cases of Impeachment shall not extend further than to removal from Office, and disqualification to hold and enjoy any Office of Honor, Trust or Profit under the United States: but the Party convicted shall nevertheless be liable and subject to Indictment, Trial, Judgment and Punishment, according to Law.

Section 4. The Times, Places and Manner of holding Elections for Senators and Representatives, shall be prescribed in each State by the Legislature thereof; but the Congress may at any time by Law make or alter such Regulations, except as to the Places of chusing Senators.

The Congress shall assemble at least once in every Year, and such Meeting shall be on the first Monday in December, unless they shall by Law appoint a different Day.

Section 5. Each House shall be the Judge of the Elections, Returns and Qualifications of its own Members, and a Majority of each shall constitute a Quorum to do Business; but a smaller Number may adjourn from day to day, and may be authorized to compel the Attendance of absent Members, in such Manner, and under such Penalties as each House may provide.

Each House may determine the Rules of its Proceedings, punish its Members for disorderly Behaviour, and, with the Concurrence of two thirds, expel a Member.

Each House shall keep a Journal of its Proceedings, and from time to time publish the same, excepting such Parts as may in their Judgment require Secrecy; and the Yeas and Nays of the Members of either House on any question shall, at the Desire of one fifth of those Present, be entered on the Journal.

Neither House, during the Session of Congress, shall, without the Consent of the other, adjourn for more than three days, nor to any other Place than that in which the two Houses shall be sitting.

Section 6. The Senators and Representatives shall receive a Compensation for their Services, to be ascertained by Law, and paid out of the Treasury of the United States. They shall in all Cases, except Treason, Felony and Breach of the Peace, be privileged from Arrest during their Attendance at the Session of their respective Houses, and in going to and returning from the same; and for any Speech or Debate in either House, they shall not be questioned in any other Place.

No Senator or Representative shall, during the Time for which he was elected, be appointed to any civil Office under the Authority of the United States, which shall have been created, or the Emoluments whereof shall have been encreased during such time: and no Person holding any Office under the United States, shall be a Member of either House during his Continuance in Office.

Section 7. All Bills for raising Revenue shall originate in the House of Representatives; but the Senate may propose or concur with Amendments as on other Bills.

Every Bill which shall have passed the House of Representatives and the Senate, shall, before it become a Law, be presented to the President of the United States; if he approve he shall sign it, but if not he shall return it, with his Objections to that House in which it shall have originated, who shall enter the Objections at large on their Journal, and proceed to reconsider it. If after such Reconsideration two thirds of that House shall agree to pass the Bill, it shall be sent, together with the Objections, to the other House, by which it shall likewise be reconsidered, and if approved by two thirds of that House, it shall become a Law. But in all such Cases the Votes of both Houses shall be determined by Yeas and Nays, and the Names of the Persons voting for and against the Bill shall be entered on the Journal of each House respectively. If any Bill shall not be returned by the President within ten Days (Sundays excepted) after it shall have been presented to him, the Same shall be a Law, in like Manner as if he had signed it, unless the Congress by their Adjournment prevent its Return, in which Case it shall not be a Law.

Every Order, Resolution, or Vote to which the Concurrence of the Senate and House of Representatives may be necessary (except on a question of Adjournment) shall be presented to the President of the United States; and before the Same shall take Effect, shall be approved by him, or being disapproved by him, shall be repassed by two thirds of the Senate and House of Representatives, according to the Rules and Limitations prescribed in the Case of a Bill.

Section 8. The Congress shall have Power To lay and collect Taxes, Duties, Imposts and Excises, to pay the Debts and provide for the common Defence and general Welfare of the United States; but all Duties, Imposts and Excises shall be uniform throughout the United States;

To borrow Money on the credit of the United States;

To regulate Commerce with foreign Nations, and among the several States, and with the Indian Tribes;

To establish an uniform Rule of Naturalization, and uniform Laws on the subject of Bankruptcies throughout the United States;

To coin Money, regulate the Value thereof, and of foreign Coin, and fix the Standard of Weights and Measures;

To provide for the Punishment of counterfeiting the Securities and current Coin of the United States;

To establish Post Offices and post Roads;

To promote the Progress of Science and useful Arts, by securing for limited Times to Authors and Inventors the exclusive Right to their respective Writings and Discoveries;

To constitute Tribunals inferior to the supreme Court;

To define and punish Piracies and Felonies committed on the high Seas, and Offences against the Law of Nations;

To declare War, grant Letters of Marque and Reprisal, and make Rules concerning Captures on Land and Water;

To raise and support Armies, but no Appropriation of Money to that Use shall be for a longer Term than two Years;

To provide and maintain a Navy;

To make Rules for the Government and Regulation of the land and the naval Forces;

To provide for calling forth the Militia to execute the Laws of the Union, suppress Insurrections and repel Invasions;

To provide for organizing, arming, and disciplining, the Militia, and for governing such Part of them as may be employed in the Service of the United States, reserving to the States respectively, the Appointment of the Officers, and the Authority of training the Militia according to the discipline prescribed by Congress;

To exercise exclusive Legislation in all Cases whatsoever, over such District (not exceeding ten Miles square) as may, by Cession of particular States, and the Acceptance of Congress, become the Seat of the Government of the United States, and to exercise like Authority over all Places purchased by the Consent of the Legislature of the State in which the Same shall be, for the Erection of Forts, Magazines, Arsenals, dock-Yards, and other needful Buildings; –And to make all Laws which shall be necessary and proper for carrying into Execution the foregoing Powers, and all other Powers vested by this Constitution in the Government of the United States, or in any Department or Officer thereof.

Section 9. The Migration or Importation of such Persons as any of the States now existing shall think proper to admit, shall not be prohibited by the Congress prior to the Year one thousand eight hundred and eight, but a Tax or duty may be imposed on such Importation, not exceeding ten dollars for each Person.

The Privilege of the Writ of Habeas Corpus shall not be suspended, unless when in Cases of Rebellion or Invasion the public Safety may require it.

No Bill of Attainder or ex post facto Law shall be passed.

No Capitation, or other direct, Tax shall be laid, unless in Proportion to the Census or Enumeration herein before directed to be taken.

No Tax or Duty shall be laid on Articles exported from any State.

No Preference shall be given by any Regulation of Commerce or Revenue to the Ports of one State over those of another: nor shall Vessels bound to, or from, one State, be obliged to enter, clear or pay Duties in another.

No Money shall be drawn from the Treasury, but in Consequence of Appropriations made by Law; and a regular Statement and Account of Receipts and Expenditures of all public Money shall be published from time to time.

No Title of Nobility shall be granted by the United States: And no Person holding any Office of Profit or Trust under them, shall, without the Consent of the Congress, accept of any present, Emolument, Office, or Title, of any kind whatever, from any King, Prince, or foreign State.

Section 10. No State shall enter into any Treaty, Alliance, or Confederation; grant Letters of Marque and Reprisal; coin Money; emit Bills of Credit; make any Thing but gold and silver Coin a Tender in Payment of Debts; pass any Bill of Attainder, ex post facto Law, or Law impairing the Obligation of Contracts, or grant any Title of Nobility.

No State shall, without the Consent of the Congress, lay any Imposts or Duties on Imports or Exports, except what may be absolutely necessary for executing it's inspection Laws: and the net Produce of all Duties and Imposts, laid by any State on Imports or Exports, shall be for the Use of the Treasury of the United States; and all such Laws shall be subject to the Revision and Controul of the Congress.

No State shall, without the Consent of Congress, lay any Duty of Tonnage, keep Troops, or Ships of War in time of Peace, enter into any Agreement or Compact with another State, or with a foreign Power, or engage in War, unless actually invaded, or in such imminent Danger as will not admit of delay.

Article II

Section 1. The executive Power shall be vested in a President of the United States of America. He shall hold his Office during the Term of four Years, and, together with the Vice President, chosen for the same Term, be elected, as follows:

Each State shall appoint, in such Manner as the Legislature thereof may direct, a Number of Electors, equal to the whole Number of Senators and Representatives to which the State may be entitled in the Congress: but no Senator or Representative, or Person holding an Office of Trust or Profit under the United States, shall be appointed an Elector.

The Electors shall meet in their respective States, and vote by Ballot for two Persons, of whom one at least shall not be an Inhabitant of the same State with themselves. And they shall make a List of all the Persons voted for, and of the Number of Votes for each; which List they shall sign and certify, and transmit sealed to the Seat of the Government of the United States, directed to the President of the Senate. The President of the Senate shall, in the Presence of the Senate and House of Representatives, open all the Certificates, and the Votes shall then be counted. The Person having the greatest Number of Votes shall be the President, if such Number be a Majority of the whole Number of Electors appointed; and if there be more than one who have such Majority, and have an equal Number of Votes, then the House of Representatives shall immediately chuse by Ballot one of them for President; and if no Person have a Majority, then from the five highest on the List the said House shall in like Manner chuse the President. But in chusing the President, the Votes shall be taken by States, the Representation from each State having one Vote; A quorum for this Purpose shall consist of a Member or Members from two thirds of the States, and a Majority of all the States shall be necessary to a Choice. In every Case, after the Choice of the President, the Person having the greatest Number of Votes of the Electors shall be the Vice President. But if there should remain two or more who have equal Votes, the Senate shall chuse from them by Ballot the Vice President.

The Congress may determine the Time of chusing the Electors, and the Day on which they shall give their Votes; which Day shall be the same throughout the United States.

No Person except a natural born Citizen, or a Citizen of the United States, at the time of the Adoption of this Constitution, shall be eligible to the Office of President; neither shall any Person be eligible to that Office who shall not have attained to the Age of thirty five Years, and been fourteen Years a Resident within the United States.

In Case of the Removal of the President from Office, or of his Death, Resignation, or Inability to discharge the Powers and Duties of the said Office, the Same shall devolve on the Vice President, and the Congress may by Law provide for the Case of Removal, Death, Resignation or Inability, both of the President and Vice President, declaring what Officer shall then act as President, and such Officer shall act accordingly, until the Disability be removed, or a President shall be elected.

The President shall, at stated Times, receive for his Services, a Compensation, which shall neither be encreased nor diminished during the Period for which he shall have been elected, and he shall not receive within that Period any other Emolument from the United States, or any of them.

Before he enter on the Execution of his Office, he shall take the following Oath or Affirmation: −"I do solemnly swear (or affirm) that I will faithfully execute the Office of President of the United States, and will to the best of my Ability, preserve, protect and defend the Constitution of the United States."

Section 2. The President shall be Commander in Chief of the Army and Navy of the United States, and of the Militia of the several States, when called into the actual Service of the United States; he may require the Opinion, in writing, of the principal Officer in each of the executive Departments, upon any Subject relating to the Duties of their respective Offices, and he shall have Power to grant Reprieves and Pardons for Offences against the United States, except in Cases of Impeachment.

He shall have Power, by and with the Advice and Consent of the Senate, to make Treaties, provided two thirds of the Senators present concur; and he shall nominate, and by and with the Advice and Consent of the Senate, shall appoint Ambassadors, other public Ministers and Consuls, Judges of the supreme Court, and all other Officers of the United States, whose

Appointments are not herein otherwise provided for, and which shall be established by Law: but the Congress may by Law vest the Appointment of such inferior Officers, as they think proper, in the President alone, in the Courts of Law, or in the Heads of Departments.

The President shall have Power to fill up all Vacancies that may happen during the Recess of the Senate, by granting Commissions which shall expire at the End of their next Session.

Section 3. He shall from time to time give to the Congress Information of the State of the Union, and recommend to their Consideration such Measures as he shall judge necessary and expedient; he may, on extraordinary Occasions, convene both Houses, or either of them, and in Case of Disagreement between them, with Respect to the Time of Adjournment, he may adjourn them to such Time as he shall think proper; he shall receive Ambassadors and other public Ministers; he shall take Care that the Laws be faithfully executed, and shall Commission all the Officers of the United States.

Section 4. The President, Vice President and all civil Officers of the United States, shall be removed from Office on Impeachment for, and Conviction of, Treason, Bribery, or other high Crimes and Misdemeanors.

Article III

Section 1. The judicial Power of the United States, shall be vested in one supreme Court, and in such inferior Courts as the Congress may from time to time ordain and establish. The Judges, both of the supreme and inferior Courts, shall hold their Offices during good Behaviour, and shall, at stated Times, receive for their Services, a Compensation, which shall not be diminished during their Continuance in Office.

Section 2. The judicial Power shall extend to all Cases, in Law and Equity, arising under this Constitution, the Laws of the United States, and Treaties made, or which shall be made, under their Authority; –to all Cases affecting Ambassadors, other public Ministers and Consuls; –to all Cases of admiralty and maritime Jurisdiction; –to Controversies to which the United States shall be a Party; –to Controversies between two or more States; –between a State and Citizens of another State; –between Citizens of different States; –between Citizens of the same State claiming Lands under Grants of different States, and between a State, or the Citizens thereof, and foreign States, Citizens or Subjects.

In all Cases affecting Ambassadors, other public Ministers and Consuls, and those in which a State shall be Party, the supreme Court shall have original Jurisdiction. In all the other Cases before mentioned, the supreme Court shall have appellate Jurisdiction, both as to Law and Fact, with such Exceptions, and under such Regulations as the Congress shall make.

The Trial of all Crimes, except in Cases of Impeachment, shall be by Jury; and such Trial shall be held in the State where the said Crimes shall have been committed; but when not committed within any State, the Trial shall be at such Place or Places as the Congress may by Law have directed.

Section 3. Treason against the United States, shall consist only in levying War against them, or in adhering to their Enemies, giving them Aid and Comfort. No Person shall be convicted of Treason unless on the Testimony of two Witnesses to the same overt Act, or on Confession in open Court.

The Congress shall have Power to declare the Punishment of Treason, but no Attainder of Treason shall work Corruption of Blood, or Forfeiture except during the Life of the Person attainted.

Article IV

Section 1. Full Faith and Credit shall be given in each State to the public Acts, Records, and judicial Proceedings of every other State. And the Congress may by general Laws prescribe the Manner in which such Acts, Records, and Proceedings shall be proved, and the Effect thereof.

Section 2. The Citizens of each State shall be entitled to all Privileges and Immunities of Citizens in the several States.

A Person charged in any State with Treason, Felony, or other Crime, who shall flee from Justice, and be found in another State, shall on Demand of the executive Authority of the State from which he fled, be delivered up, to be removed to the State having Jurisdiction of the Crime.

No Person held to Service or Labour in one State, under the Laws thereof, escaping into another, shall, in Consequence of any Law or Regulation therein, be discharged from such Service or Labour, but shall be delivered up on Claim of the Party to whom such Service or Labour may be due.

Section 3. New States may be admitted by the Congress into this Union; but no new States shall be formed or erected within the Jurisdiction of any other State; nor any State be formed by the Junction of two or more States, or Parts of States, without the Consent of the Legislatures of the States concerned as well as of the Congress.

The Congress shall have Power to dispose of and make all needful Rules and Regulations respecting the Territory or other Property belonging to the United States; and nothing in this Constitution shall be so construed as to Prejudice any Claims of the United States, or of any particular State.

Section 4. The United States shall guarantee to every State in this Union a Republican Form of Government, and shall protect each of them against Invasion; and on Application of the Legislature, or of the Executive (when the Legislature cannot be convened) against domestic Violence.

Article V

The Congress, whenever two thirds of both Houses shall deem it necessary, shall propose Amendments to this Constitution, or, on the Application of the Legislatures of two thirds of the several States, shall call a Convention for proposing Amendments, which, in either Case, shall be valid to all Intents and Purposes, as Part of this Constitution, when ratified by the Legislatures of three fourths of the several States, or by Conventions in three fourths thereof, as the one or the other Mode of Ratification may be proposed by the Congress; Provided that no Amendment which may be made prior to the Year One thousand eight hundred and eight shall in any Manner affect the first and fourth Clauses in the Ninth Section of the first Article; and that no State, without its Consent, shall be deprived of its equal Suffrage in the Senate.

Article VI

All Debts contracted and Engagements entered into, before the Adoption of this Constitution, shall be as valid against the United States under this Constitution, as under the Confederation.

This Constitution, and the Laws of the United States which shall be made in Pursuance thereof; and all Treaties made, or which shall be made, under the Authority of the United States, shall be the supreme Law of the Land; and the Judges in every State shall be bound thereby, any Thing in the Constitution or Laws of any State to the Contrary notwith-standing.

The Senators and Representatives before mentioned, and the Members of the several State Legislatures, and all executive and judicial Officers, both of the United States and of the several States, shall be bound by Oath or Affirmation, to support this Constitution; but no religious Test shall ever be required as a Qualification to any Office or public Trust under the United States.

Article VII

The Ratification of the Conventions of nine States, shall be sufficient for the Establishment of this Constitution between the States so ratifying the Same.

Done in Convention by the Unanimous Consent of the States present the Seventeenth Day of September in the Year of our Lord one thousand seven hundred and Eighty seven and of the Independence of the United States of America the Twelfth In Witness whereof We have hereunto subscribed our Names:

G. Washington – Presid.
And deputy from Virginia

New Hampshire: John Langdon, Nicholas Gilman

Massachusetts: Nathaniel Gorham, Rufus King

Connecticut: William Samuel Johnson, Roger Sherman

New York: Alexander Hamilton

New Jersey: William Livingston, David Brearly,
William Paterson, Jonathan Dayton

Pennsylvania: Benjamin Franklin, Thomas Mifflin,
Robert Morris, George Clymer, Thomas
FitzSimons, Jared Ingersoll, James Wilson,
Gouverneur Morris

Delaware: George Read, Gunning Bedford, Jr., John
Dickinson, Richard Bassett, Jacob Broom

Maryland: James McHenry, Daniel of Saint Thomas
Jenifer, Daniel Carroll

Virginia: John Blair, James Madison, Jr.

North Carolina: William Blount, Richard Dobbs Spaight,
Hugh Williamson

South Carolina: John Rutledge, Charles Cotesworth
Pinckney, Charles Pinckney, Pierce Butler

Georgia: William Few, Abraham Baldwin

Attest William Jackson Secretary

The Preamble to The Bill of Rights

Congress of the United States begun and held at the City of New-York, on Wednesday the fourth of March, one thousand seven hundred and eighty nine.

THE Conventions of a number of the States, having at the time of their adopting the Constitution, expressed a desire, in order to prevent misconstruction or abuse of its powers, that further declaratory and restrictive clauses should be added: And as extending the ground of public confidence in the Government, will best ensure the beneficent ends of its institution.

RESOLVED by the Senate and House of Representatives of the United States of America, in Congress assembled, two thirds of both Houses concurring, that the following Articles be proposed to the Legislatures of the several States, as amendments to the Constitution of the United States, all, or any of which Articles, when ratified by three fourths of the said Legislatures, to be valid to all intents and purposes, as part of the said Constitution; viz.

ARTICLES in addition to, and Amendment of the Constitution of the United States of America, proposed by Congress, and ratified by the Legislatures of the several States, pursuant to the fifth Article of the original Constitution.

Amendment I
Congress shall make no law respecting an establishment of religion, or prohibiting the free exercise thereof; or abridging the freedom of speech, or of the press; or the right of the people peaceably to assemble, and to petition the Government for a redress of grievances.

Amendment II
A well regulated Militia, being necessary to the security of a free State, the right of the people to keep and bear Arms, shall not be infringed.

Amendment III
No Soldier shall, in time of peace be quartered in any house, without the consent of the Owner, nor in time of war, but in a manner to be prescribed by law.

Amendment IV
The right of the people to be secure in their persons, houses, papers, and effects, against unreasonable searches and seizures, shall not be violated,

and no Warrants shall issue, but upon probable cause, supported by Oath or affirmation, and particularly describing the place to be searched, and the persons or things to be seized.

Amendment V

No person shall be held to answer for a capital, or otherwise infamous crime, unless on a presentment or indictment of a Grand Jury, except in cases arising in the land or naval forces, or in the Militia, when in actual service in time of War or public danger; nor shall any person be subject for the same offence to be twice put in jeopardy of life or limb; nor shall be compelled in any criminal case to be a witness against himself, nor be deprived of life, liberty, or property, without due process of law; nor shall private property be taken for public use, without just compensation.

Amendment VI

In all criminal prosecutions, the accused shall enjoy the right to a speedy and public trial, by an impartial jury of the State and district wherein the crime shall have been committed, which district shall have been previously ascertained by law, and to be informed of the nature and cause of the accusation; to be confronted with the witnesses against him; to have compulsory process for obtaining witnesses in his favor, and to have the Assistance of Counsel for his defence.

Amendment VII

In Suits at common law, where the value in controversy shall exceed twenty dollars, the right of trial by jury shall be preserved, and no fact tried by a jury, shall be otherwise re-examined in any Court of the United States, than according to the rules of the common law.

Amendment VIII

Excessive bail shall not be required, nor excessive fines imposed, nor cruel and unusual punishments inflicted.

Amendment IX

The enumeration in the Constitution, of certain rights, shall not be construed to deny or disparage others retained by the people.

Amendment X

The powers not delegated to the United States by the Constitution, nor prohibited by it to the States, are reserved to the States respectively, or to the people.

Amendments 11-27

AMENDMENT XI
Passed by Congress March 4, 1794. Ratified February 7, 1795.

Note: Article III, section 2, of the Constitution was modified by amendment 11.

The Judicial power of the United States shall not be construed to extend to any suit in law or equity, commenced or prosecuted against one of the United States by Citizens of another State, or by Citizens or Subjects of any Foreign State.

AMENDMENT XII
Passed by Congress December 9, 1803. Ratified June 15, 1804.

Note: A portion of Article II, section 1 of the Constitution was superseded by the 12th amendment.

The Electors shall meet in their respective states and vote by ballot for President and Vice-President, one of whom, at least, shall not be an inhabitant of the same state with themselves; they shall name in their ballots the person voted for as President, and in distinct ballots the person voted for as Vice-President, and they shall make distinct lists of all persons voted for as President, and of all persons voted for as Vice-President, and of the number of votes for each, which lists they shall sign and certify, and transmit sealed to the seat of the government of the United States, directed to the President of the Senate; – the President of the Senate shall, in the presence of the Senate and House of Representatives, open all the certificates and the votes shall then be counted; – The person having the greatest number of votes for President, shall be the President, if such number be a majority of the whole number of Electors appointed; and if no person have such majority, then from the persons having the highest numbers not exceeding three on the list of those voted for as President, the House of Representatives shall choose immediately, by ballot, the President. But in choosing the President, the votes shall be taken by states, the representation from each state having one vote; a quorum for this purpose shall consist of a member or members from two-thirds of the states, and a majority of all the states shall be necessary to a choice. [And if the House of Representatives shall not choose a President whenever the right of choice shall devolve upon them, before the fourth day of March next following, then the Vice-President shall act as President, as in case of the death or other constitutional disability of the President. –]* The person having the greatest number of votes as Vice-President, shall be the Vice-President, if such number be a majority of the whole number of Electors appointed, and if no person have a majority, then from the two highest numbers on the list, the Senate shall choose the Vice-President; a quorum for the purpose shall consist of two-thirds of the whole number of Senators, and a majority of the whole number shall be necessary to a choice. But no person constitutionally ineligible to the office of President shall be eligible to that of Vice-President of the United States.

Superseded by section 3 of the 20th amendment.

AMENDMENT XIII

Passed by Congress January 31, 1865. Ratified December 6, 1865.

Note: A portion of Article IV, section 2, of the Constitution was superseded by the 13th amendment.

Section 1.
Neither slavery nor involuntary servitude, except as a punishment for crime whereof the party shall have been duly convicted, shall exist within the United States, or any place subject to their jurisdiction.

Section 2.
Congress shall have power to enforce this article by appropriate legislation.

AMENDMENT XIV

Passed by Congress June 13, 1866. Ratified July 9, 1868.

Note: Article I, section 2, of the Constitution was modified by section 2 of the 14th amendment.

Section 1.
All persons born or naturalized in the United States, and subject to the jurisdiction thereof, are citizens of the United States and of the State wherein they reside. No State shall make or enforce any law which shall abridge the privileges or immunities of citizens of the United States; nor shall any State deprive any person of life, liberty, or property, without

due process of law; nor deny to any person within its jurisdiction the equal protection of the laws.

Section 2.

Representatives shall be apportioned among the several States according to their respective numbers, counting the whole number of persons in each State, excluding Indians not taxed. But when the right to vote at any election for the choice of electors for President and Vice-President of the United States, Representatives in Congress, the Executive and Judicial officers of a State, or the members of the Legislature thereof, is denied to any of the male inhabitants of such State, being twenty-one years of age,* and citizens of the United States, or in any way abridged, except for participation in rebellion, or other crime, the basis of representation therein shall be reduced in the proportion which the number of such male citizens shall bear to the whole number of male citizens twenty-one years of age in such State.

Section 3.

No person shall be a Senator or Representative in Congress, or elector of President and Vice-President, or hold any office, civil or military, under the United States, or under any State, who, having previously taken an oath, as a member of Congress, or as an officer of the United States, or as a member of any State legislature, or as an executive or judicial officer of any State, to support the Constitution of the United States, shall have engaged in insurrection or rebellion against the same, or given aid or comfort to the enemies thereof. But Congress may by a vote of two-thirds of each House, remove such disability.

Section 4.

The validity of the public debt of the United States, authorized by law, including debts incurred for payment of pensions and bounties for services in suppressing insurrection or rebellion, shall not be questioned. But neither the United States nor any State shall assume or pay any debt or obligation incurred in aid of insurrection or rebellion against the United States, or any claim for the loss or emancipation of any slave; but all such debts, obligations and claims shall be held illegal and void.

Section 5.

The Congress shall have the power to enforce, by appropriate legislation, the provisions of this article.

Changed by section 1 of the 26th amendment.

AMENDMENT XV
Passed by Congress February 26, 1869. Ratified February 3, 1870.

Section 1.
The right of citizens of the United States to vote shall not be denied or abridged by the United States or by any State on account of race, color, or previous condition of servitude.

Section 2.
Congress shall have power to enforce this article by appropriate legislation.

AMENDMENT XVI
Passed by Congress July 2, 1909. Ratified February 3, 1913.

Note: Article I, section 9, of the Constitution was modified by the 16th amendment.

The Congress shall have power to lay and collect taxes on incomes, from whatever source derived, without apportionment among the several States, and without regard to any census or enumeration.

AMENDMENT XVII
Passed by Congress May 13, 1912. Ratified April 8, 1913.

Note: Article I, section 3, of the Constitution was modified by the 17th amendment.

The Senate of the United States shall be composed of two Senators from each State, elected by the people thereof, for six years; and each Senator shall have one vote. The electors in each State shall have the qualifications requisite for electors of the most numerous branch of the State legislatures.

When vacancies happen in the representation of any State in the Senate, the executive authority of such State shall issue writs of election to fill such vacancies: *Provided*, That the legislature of any State may empower the executive thereof to make temporary appointments until the people fill the vacancies by election as the legislature may direct.

This amendment shall not be so construed as to affect the election or term of any Senator chosen before it becomes valid as part of the Constitution.

AMENDMENT XVIII
Passed by Congress December 18, 1917. Ratified January 16, 1919. Repealed by amendment 21.

Section 1.
After one year from the ratification of this article the manufacture, sale, or transportation of intoxicating liquors within, the importation thereof into, or the exportation thereof from the United States and all territory subject to the jurisdiction thereof for beverage purposes is hereby prohibited.

Section 2.
The Congress and the several States shall have concurrent power to enforce this article by appropriate legislation.

Section 3.
This article shall be inoperative unless it shall have been ratified as an amendment to the Constitution by the legislatures of the several States, as provided in the Constitution, within seven years from the date of the submission hereof to the States by the Congress.

AMENDMENT XIX
Passed by Congress June 4, 1919. Ratified August 18, 1920.

The right of citizens of the United States to vote shall not be denied or abridged by the United States or by any State on account of sex. Congress shall have power to enforce this article by appropriate legislation.

AMENDMENT XX
Passed by Congress March 2, 1932. Ratified January 23, 1933.

Note: Article I, section 4, of the Constitution was modified by section 2 of this amendment. In addition, a portion of the 12th amendment was superseded by section 3.

Section 1.
The terms of the President and the Vice President shall end at noon on the 20th day of January, and the terms of Senators and Representatives at noon on the 3d day of January, of the years in which such terms would have ended if this article had not been ratified; and the terms of their successors shall then begin.

Section 2.

The Congress shall assemble at least once in every year, and such meeting shall begin at noon on the 3d day of January, unless they shall by law appoint a different day.

Section 3.

If, at the time fixed for the beginning of the term of the President, the President elect shall have died, the Vice President elect shall become President. If a President shall not have been chosen before the time fixed for the beginning of his term, or if the President elect shall have failed to qualify, then the Vice President elect shall act as President until a President shall have qualified; and the Congress may by law provide for the case wherein neither a President elect nor a Vice President shall have qualified, declaring who shall then act as President, or the manner in which one who is to act shall be selected, and such person shall act accordingly until a President or Vice President shall have qualified.

Section 4.

The Congress may by law provide for the case of the death of any of the persons from whom the House of Representatives may choose a President whenever the right of choice shall have devolved upon them, and for the case of the death of any of the persons from whom the Senate may choose a Vice President whenever the right of choice shall have devolved upon them.

Section 5.

Sections 1 and 2 shall take effect on the 15th day of October following the ratification of this article.

Section 6.

This article shall be inoperative unless it shall have been ratified as an amendment to the Constitution by the legislatures of three-fourths of the several States within seven years from the date of its submission.

AMENDMENT XXI

Passed by Congress February 20, 1933. Ratified December 5, 1933.

Section 1.

The eighteenth article of amendment to the Constitution of the United States is hereby repealed.

Section 2.
The transportation or importation into any State, Territory, or Possession of the United States for delivery or use therein of intoxicating liquors, in violation of the laws thereof, is hereby prohibited.

Section 3.
This article shall be inoperative unless it shall have been ratified as an amendment to the Constitution by conventions in the several States, as provided in the Constitution, within seven years from the date of the submission hereof to the States by the Congress.

AMENDMENT XXII
Passed by Congress March 21, 1947. Ratified February 27, 1951.

Section 1.
No person shall be elected to the office of the President more than twice, and no person who has held the office of President, or acted as President, for more than two years of a term to which some other person was elected President shall be elected to the office of President more than once. But this Article shall not apply to any person holding the office of President when this Article was proposed by Congress, and shall not prevent any person who may be holding the office of President, or acting as President, during the term within which this Article becomes operative from holding the office of President or acting as President during the remainder of such term.

Section 2.
This article shall be inoperative unless it shall have been ratified as an amendment to the Constitution by the legislatures of three-fourths of the several States within seven years from the date of its submission to the States by the Congress.

AMENDMENT XXIII
Passed by Congress June 16, 1960. Ratified March 29, 1961.

Section 1.
The District constituting the seat of Government of the United States shall appoint in such manner as Congress may direct:

A number of electors of President and Vice President equal to the whole number of Senators and Representatives in Congress to which the District would be entitled if it were a State, but in no event more than the least populous State; they shall be in addition to those appointed by the States, but they shall be considered, for the purposes of the election of President and Vice President, to be electors appointed by a State; and they shall meet in the District and perform such duties as provided by the twelfth article of amendment.

Section 2.
Congress shall have power to enforce this article by appropriate legislation.

AMENDMENT XXIV
Passed by Congress August 27, 1962. Ratified January 23, 1964.

Section 1.
The right of citizens of the United States to vote in any primary or other election for President or Vice President, for electors for President or Vice President, or for Senator or Representative in Congress, shall not be denied or abridged by the United States or any State by reason of failure to pay poll tax or other tax.

Section 2.
Congress shall have power to enforce this article by appropriate legislation.

AMENDMENT XXV
Passed by Congress July 6, 1965. Ratified February 10, 1967.

Note: Article II, section 1, of the Constitution was affected by the 25th amendment.

Section 1.
In case of the removal of the President from office or of his death or resignation, the Vice President shall become President.

Section 2.
Whenever there is a vacancy in the office of the Vice President, the President shall nominate a Vice President who shall take office upon confirmation by a majority vote of both Houses of Congress.

Section 3.

Whenever the President transmits to the President pro tempore of the Senate and the Speaker of the House of Representatives his written declaration that he is unable to discharge the powers and duties of his office, and until he transmits to them a written declaration to the contrary, such powers and duties shall be discharged by the Vice President as Acting President.

Section 4.

Whenever the Vice President and a majority of either the principal officers of the executive departments or of such other body as Congress may by law provide, transmit to the President pro tempore of the Senate and the Speaker of the House of Representatives their written declaration that the President is unable to discharge the powers and duties of his office, the Vice President shall immediately assume the powers and duties of the office as Acting President.

Thereafter, when the President transmits to the President pro tempore of the Senate and the Speaker of the House of Representatives his written declaration that no inability exists, he shall resume the powers and duties of his office unless the Vice President and a majority of either the principal officers of the executive department or of such other body as Congress may by law provide, transmit within four days to the President pro tempore of the Senate and the Speaker of the House of Representatives their written declaration that the President is unable to discharge the powers and duties of his office. Thereupon Congress shall decide the issue, assembling within forty-eight hours for that purpose if not in session. If the Congress, within twenty-one days after receipt of the latter written declaration, or, if Congress is not in session, within twenty-one days after Congress is required to assemble, determines by two-thirds vote of both Houses that the President is unable to discharge the powers and duties of his office, the Vice President shall continue to discharge the same as Acting President; otherwise, the President shall resume the powers and duties of his office.

AMENDMENT XXVI

Passed by Congress March 23, 1971. Ratified July 1, 1971.

Note: Amendment 14, section 2, of the Constitution was modified by section 1 of the 26th amendment.

Section 1.
The right of citizens of the United States, who are eighteen years of age or older, to vote shall not be denied or abridged by the United States or by any State on account of age.

Section 2.
Congress shall have power to enforce this article by appropriate legislation.

AMENDMENT XXVII

Originally proposed Sept. 25, 1789. Ratified May 7, 1992.

No law, varying the compensation for the services of the Senators and Representatives, shall take effect, until an election of representatives shall have intervened.

ABOUT THE AUTHOR

Paul Curtman enlisted in the United States Marine Corp and served his country as an infantryman with Golf Co. 2nd Battalion 3rd Marines. While stationed in Hawaii, Paul became a Marine Corp Martial Arts Instructor and was instrumental in teaching infantry Marines hand-to-hand combat. As a Sergeant in the Marines, Paul participated, as a squad leader, in support of Operation Enduring Freedom.

After leaving active duty, Paul continued his service as a Marine Reservist for another six years. While in the Marine Reserves, Paul attended the University of Missouri St. Louis where he earned a Bachelor's degree in Political Science. Following graduation from the University, Paul became a licensed Series 7 Investment Representative.

Paul is an ardent student of history and supporter of the United States Constitution. His outspoken and public advocacy for our elected leaders to adhere, and be responsive to the will of the people and the United States Constitution has resulted in numerous appearances on both local and national television and talk radio shows.

First and foremost, Paul believes that sound principles are the cornerstone of good government. He has said on numerous occasions "elected office is to be reserved as a seat of service, not a seat of status: seats reserved for statesmen not politicians."

www.paulcurtman.com